Introducing commerce

Englanf.
Earth.
Galaxy 2.

Introducing commerce

Second edition

Rosemary Wells
and Cindy Ferguson

LONGMAN GROUP UK LIMITED
Longman House, Burnt Mill, Harlow, Essex CM20 2JE, UK
and Associated Companies throughout the World.

First published 1982
Second edition 1987
Second impression 1987

ISBN 0 582 22500 0

Set in 10/12pt Times Roman, Linotron 202

Produced by Longman Group (FE) Ltd
Printed in Hong Kong

Contents

Acknowledgements

We are grateful to the following for permission to reproduce photographs:

Abbey National Building Society, page 177; Access, the Joint Credit Card Company Limited, page 170 below; Aerofilms Limited, page 89; The Association of British Travel Agents, page 190 below; ATA Stockholm, page 17; Barclays Bank plc, pages 55, 63 below, 171 above and below; The Baltic Exchange, page 162; Barnaby's Picture Library, page, 4 below, 11, 23, 87; Birds Eye Wall's Limited, page 183 left; BiS (Banking Information Service), pages 60 above, 68, 69 below right, 70, 74, 75 left and right; Brenard Press Limited, page 132 above; British Library, page 18; British Rail, pages 132 below, 157 above left and right, 157 below left; British Standards Institution, page 191 below; British Electrotechnical Approvals Board, page 190 centre; British Waterways Board, page 160; Lance Browne, page 179; J. Allan Cash, pages, 52 below, 53; Central Electricity Generating Board, page 132 centre; Chelmsford Co-operative Society Limited, page 130 right; Clarks, page 100 above; T. Clifford, page 180 above; Comet, page 37; Consumer's Association, page 193; Co-operative Wholesale Society Limited, page 130 left; Covent Garden Market Authority, pages 43, 52 above; Crown Copyright. By permission of the Controller of Her Majesty's Stationery Office, pages 85, 108; The Design Council, page 191 centre; Diners Club International, page 171 below; Emery Worldwide, pages 164 below, 165; Erith plc, page 119 below; Mary Evans Picture Library, pages 24, 119 below; Ford Motor Company Limited, pages 1, 129; Freemans, page 35 above; Freightliner Limited, page 154; General Accident Insurance, page 95; Hamlet Furniture Limited, page 49 right; International Wool Secretariat, page 190 above; P. & P.F. James, page 151; Guy Laroche, page 182; John Lewis Partnership, pages 47, 71; The Littlewoods Organisation, pages 34 centre, 34 right; Lloyds Bank plc, pages 59 above, 64; Lloyd's of London, pages 102 below, 103; Massey-Ferguson (U.K.) Limited, page 100 below left; Midland Bank plc, pages 58 right, 63 centre, 65; National Coal Board, page 157 below right; National Girobank, pages 69 below left, 79, 80, 81, 82, 83; National Westminster Bank plc, pages 62, 63 above, 67; Nationwide Building Society, page 177; Neatwear Tie Company Limited, page 35 below; Orkney Island Council, page 13; Peake Freight Services Limited, page 155 below; Pearl Assurance plc, pages 90, 99; Pearson, pages 118 below, 119 above; Photosource, pages 9, 40 centre, 48, 49 above left, 49 below left, 153 left, 170 above, 171 below; Pickfords Removals Limited, page 159; Pifco, page 5 above; Popperfoto, page 107; Port of London Authority, pages 155 above, 161; The Post Office, pages 77, 84, 85; Provident Personal Credit Limited, page 169; Rowenta (U.K.) Limited, page 197; Sainsbury's, page 138; SEGAS, page 78; Smith & Nephew Associated Companies plc, pages 124, 125; The Stock Photobank – London, page 126 above and below; Syndication International, page 208 below; Thorn EMI Rental Services Ltd, page 60 below; TSB Trustcard, page 73; Topham, page 8; Tupperware, page 40 above; UTA French Airlines, page 164 above; Wimpy International Limited, page 30; Woolwich, page 177. Cover: Queensgate Shopping Centre, Peterborough Development Corporation (photo: Roger Austin)

Foreword to teachers

This book is designed for the GCSE pupil of Commerce, Social Studies and Social Economics, who finds difficulty in absorbing a whole chapter of the more traditional text book.

All too often a text book chapter does not fall into convenient sections that correspond with the structure and pace of lessons. Here, each main chapter is divided into topic units, each contained on a double-page spread, suitable for one lesson. The pupil never has to read more than a few paragraphs before testing his or her understanding. Questions, which are identified by **Q1**, **Q2**, etc. are linked not only to the text, but to a profusion of diagrams, photographs and drawings. Vocabulary is carefully graded as to age and ability; and a variety of teaching approaches, from strip cartoons onwards, enlivens the learning process for the child.

For the teacher, here is the equivalent of worksheets immediately to hand on each aspect of the GCSE Commerce syllabus — to be used as classwork; set as homework; or available for classes when the teacher is absent!

1 Production and trade

The study of commerce explores the everyday business world of which you will be a part when you leave school. Trade is essential to all our lives: and many services have been developed to help us trade all over the world. Trade and aids-to-trade is what is meant by **Commerce.** The commercial services of banking, insurance, transport etc, are used by individuals in their private lives, as well as in business. What you learn here will certainly be of use to you later and it will give you confidence to have studied it.

Sections
1. Production of goods
2. Production of services   Consumer goods   Capital goods
3. From producer to consumer   Pattern of distribution
4. Division of labour
5. Location of industry
6. Specialisation Regional policy
7. Chain of production   Money-go-round
8. Barter and money
9. The development of Britain's trade   The EEC
10. Foreign trade   Balance of Trade   Balance of Payments

Section 1

Production of goods

People work, firstly, to keep themselves and their families alive; and then to make life more pleasant. The type of work and the type of production that people are engaged in depends on where they live, and on how well developed production and trade are in the society in which they live.

Primary production uses the basic gifts of Nature, e.g. by farming, hunting, mining. These are called **extractive** industries because they draw out from the earth or sea raw materials for the production of goods.

Manufacture is the making of goods from raw materials with the aid of tools and machinery. Primitive people used muscle, or animals, waterpower and wind to help drive machines. It was only the development of steam-power, however, that brought about mass-production by power-driven machinery.

Assembly is the name given to production whereby goods are made not from raw materials, but from manufactured parts, e.g. car assembly.

Construction is the name given to the production of houses, roads, bridges, i.e. things 'built'.

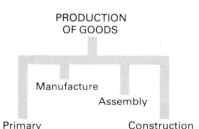

PRODUCTION OF GOODS

Manufacture

Assembly

Primary or extractive industry

Construction

Q1 Copy the diagram.

Q2 Place the following occupations under the correct heading in your diagram:

textile weaver
road repairer
nuts and bolt maker
baker
lumberjack

bricklayer
typewriter engineer
mechanic in tractor factory
civil engineer designing a bridge
North Sea Oil driller

Q3 Transport is necessary for the development of trade. List the types of transport that might be used by people in the society illustrated in each of the pictures on these two pages.

A farmer may grow more tomatoes than his family eats. He will want to take his extra tomatoes to the local market to trade his surplus for other goods.

Production of goods intended just for sale, rather than use by the producer, is called "**production for the market**". The term **market** is used to describe any getting together of buyers and sellers. The price at which goods are sold in any market depends on how high the seller thinks he can go. Rare or scarce goods will tend to be expensive. Keen competition may keep prices down. The seller, of course, has to cover his costs to stay in trade.

Trade in beautiful and unusual goods — shells, gold and jewellery — developed a long time ago, even across mountains and seas.

Q4 What is meant by the term "market"?

Q5 What is meant by the expression "production for the market"?

Q6 What decides the price at which goods are sold in the market?

Q7 Which raw materials are needed for the following manufactured goods:

furniture	bath towels	tyres
biscuits	blankets	

Q8 Give four manufactured items used in the construction of a house.

Q9 Give three manufactured parts used in a car assembly line.

Section 2

Production of services

In a society with developed production and trade, people take it for granted that they can buy many **services** as well as goods. Insurance brokers or estate agents work from "shops", for example, as do hairdressers. Transport services are sold by ticket, as is entertainment.

The higher the standard of living, the more services are supplied. The term production is used in Commerce for anything for which others are prepared to pay, i.e. for services as well as goods. Those buying goods and services are called **consumers**.

Service industries include the hairdressing industry, the news industry, the catering industry, the entertainment industry, the sports industry, the passenger transport industry, and other services on sale to the general public.

Q1 Give four examples of services sold from shops in the High Street.

Q2 Give four examples of services providing for leisure and enjoyment.

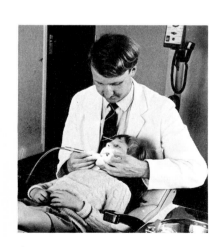

Direct services cover people who are professionally trained to help individuals personally, e.g. doctors, dentists, teachers, solicitors, etc.

Q3 Name professional people in Direct Services to whom you would go for:
  a) advice about the law
  b) help with exercise after a major operation
  c) consultation about accounts, for tax purposes.

As production and trade increase so the number of services develop that aid trade, e.g. banking, insurance, market research, advertising. These are called **Commercial Services**.

PRODUCTION OF
SERVICES

Service industries — Direct services — Commercial services

Q4 Name the commercial service of:
a) storing goods before sale
b) transferring goods by ship between countries
c) letting the public know about goods available
d) providing foreign currencies
e) questioning people to find out their views on products.

Q5 Copy the diagram opposite.

Q6 Place the following occupations under the correct heading in your diagram:

journalist	bus conductor	bank clerk
nurse	pop singer	door-to-door salesman
lawyer	waiter	producer of TV commercials
	surgeon	

Consumer goods

The **consumer goods** industry is concerned with producing goods bought and used by the general public, e.g. foods, furniture, clothes, domestic appliances, etc. Consumer goods may be **perishables**, e.g. vegetables; or consumer **durables**, e.g. washing-machines; or **non-durables** such as clothing and other textile goods.

Capital goods

The **capital goods** industry is concerned with manufacturing durables, e.g. machinery, equipment and vehicles, which firms use again and again, and are not for resale.

Q7 What are consumer goods?

Q8 Give five examples each of:
a) perishable consumer goods
b) durable consumer goods
c) non-durable consumer goods.

Q9 What are capital goods?

Q10 Give five examples of capital goods owned by firms to use again and again in the course of their business.

Section 3

From producer to consumer

Goods and services are produced in order to be sold. **Commerce** is the name given to trade and to the services that help trade. Commerce is therefore concerned with the distribution and exchange of goods and services.

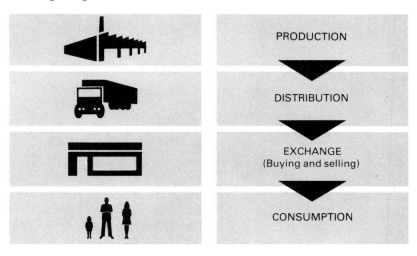

Distribution covers getting goods from the producer to the consumer. It could include not only transport, but the organisation of warehouses and shops stocking goods.

Exchange covers the buying and selling of goods and services, i.e. goods are exchanged for money and money is exchanged for goods.

At each stage between the production of raw materials, the manufacture of goods and their final sale to the consumer, the services of banking, insurance and transport are used. The more trade develops, the more services are produced as **aids-to-trade**, e.g. storage, advertising, market research, packaging, display. All these are Commercial Services: Commerce is trade and aids-to-trade.

COMMERCE

Trade   Aids-to-trade

Home   Overseas

Q1 What is meant by Distribution?

Q2 What is meant by Exchange?

Q3 Name three commercial services which are used at each stage between the production of raw materials and the final sale of goods to the consumer.

Q4 Copy the diagram above and complete it by naming eight aids-to-trade.

Pattern of Distribution
Between the producer and consumer may be many layers of buyers and sellers.

MANUFACTURER OR PRODUCER Selling in bulk

WHOLESALER Selling in large quantities

RETAILER Selling in small quantities

CONSUMER

Commodity Markets, or Exchanges, are markets for raw materials, organised on a world-wide basis to supply manufacturers. For example,
from mines (tin, copper, zinc, diamonds)
from farms and plantations $\left[\begin{array}{l}\text{food — tea, cocoa beans, wheat, barley}\\\text{fibres — wool, cotton, jute, flax, rubber}\end{array}\right]$

Manufacturers buy raw materials from commodity markets and sell **in bulk** to wholesalers who are part of the **pattern of distribution**. To **wholesale** means to sell in large quantities, e.g. to shops, the next step in the pattern of distribution.

Wholesale markets supply perishable goods, e.g. fruit and vegetables, meat and fish to shops, hotels, restaurants and hospitals.

Retail means to sell in small quantities, i.e. to the consumer. Retailing includes not only shops but street markets, mail order, slot machines etc.

Q5 What is a Commodity Exchange? Give five examples.
Q6 What is meant by Wholesaling? To whom do wholesalers distribute goods?
Q7 Why do shops obtain tinned vegetables from wholesale warehouses, but fresh vegetables from wholesale markets?
Q8 a) What is meant by retailing?
b) Give three examples.
c) To whom do retailers distribute goods?
Q9 Draw the Pattern of Distribution diagram above.

Section 4

Division of labour

Robinson Crusoe, alone on his desert island, had to do all jobs himself. Some he might do well; some he might do badly; but what he could not do was left undone. Today, nobody expects to be self-sufficient.

Division of labour is the breaking down of each job or trade into small tasks done by different people. An isolated farm family would at one time grow their own crops; butcher their animals for food; make their own candles and soap; weave cloth and sew their own clothes. Then, with division of labour, specialist trades developed. A village might have its own butcher, shoemaker, weaver and tailor. Division of labour led to greater skill and greater speed at particular jobs, to better quality and a greater quantity of output. Also, more types of job developed as production and trade expanded, and people had more choice of what to do, and what job best suited their talents. Overall, more goods produced meant a lower cost for each article; people could afford to buy more; and the standard of living rose.

In our society, raw materials are produced by one set of workers; manufactured parts by another set; and the parts are assembled for finished articles by yet a different group. Within each group there may be dozens of different processes. Someone may work at a particular process as part of a production line, without ever seeing or using the finished product. We are **inter-dependent**. We depend on others for production of the goods we need and use.

If the stages on a production line are divided into a sequence of simple jobs, less training is needed, and unskilled (cheaper) labour can be employed. Workers may find their repetitive tasks boring, and their work lacking in **job satisfaction**. Here the division of labour or **specialisation** causes problems. Also, with the development of new processes and techniques, a worker may find that his/her specialist skill is no longer needed, and face unemployment and the need for re-training.

Q1 Make a numbered list of advantages gained from the division of labour. Can you add others not mentioned above?

Q2 Make a numbered list of disadvantages from applying the division of labour or specialisation. Can you add others not mentioned above?

Q3 Choosing any place of work you know, show the division of labour by naming three different jobs there, with a paragraph describing each.

Jobs may be called "skilled" or "unskilled" according to the amount of training required. "Manual" work refers to practical jobs requiring physical effort, whereas office jobs are called "non-manual" or "white-collar" work. The number of "white-collar" workers rises in a country with a high standard of living, as people can afford to pay for many more services, such as holiday tours, entertainment, sport and dry-cleaning. Division of labour has

enabled more goods to be produced and traded so markets expand. The production for large markets leads to **large-scale production** using production processes employing many workers doing simple tasks assisted by machinery. This is called **mechanisation**. Recently factories have been built where the machines (or robots) do all the work, controlled by computer, and just a handful of workers control the programmes and watch the dials. This is called **automation**.

Large-scale production or **mass-production** has brought the majority of people goods that they could not have afforded if made by individual craftsmen, e.g. refrigerators, televisions, motor cars. So mass-production has enabled the "masses" to enjoy a higher standard of living. Yet it is often criticised for the "sameness" or standardisation of products it creates; and for the disappearance of skilled craftsmen.

Q4 List three manual, unskilled jobs; three manual skilled jobs; and three white collar jobs.

Q5 What is the difference between mechanisation and automation?

Q6 What is the benefit of large-scale production?

Q7 Explain why mass-production is criticised.

Section 5

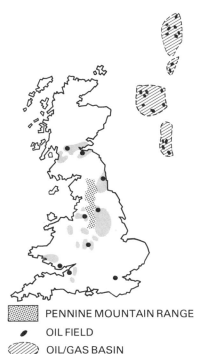

▨ PENNINE MOUNTAIN RANGE

● OIL FIELD

▨ OIL/GAS BASIN

▨ COALFIELDS

● MAIN POPULATION CENTRES

Location of industry

The siting of towns and villages followed some natural advantage, such as the availability of fresh water and easy access. Villages often grew around castles which guarded land or sea routes and offered protection and employment. A good harbour, or a place where road or waterway routes met, was a natural location for a trading settlement. The presence of mineral wealth led to the growth of mining industries etc.

In Britain the pattern of industrial towns was set during the Industrial Revolution. The new machines needed a source of power, so towns grew up near coalmines, as this source of power is heavy and expensive to transport. The cotton industry developed in Lancashire on the west of the Pennine mountains where the wet winds suited cotton spinning and weaving, and raw cotton could be easily imported through good ports. Wool requires a drier atmosphere, and the mills were located on the east, or lee side of the mountains, using wool from British flocks. The engineering towns of the Midlands grew up where coal and iron deposits were found close together. Our coalmining, chemical, shipbuilding and fishing industries used the natural advantages of the earth and sea.

More recently, the discovery of oil has caused the development of new concentrations of industries around our coastline. Many of the oilfields are under the sea and require large amounts of engineering work and supplies of all types, and transport for the many workers stationed on the oil rigs.

Q1 Give three reasons for the siting of settlements.

Q2 Give three natural advantages influencing the location of industry in Britain.

Q3 Think of and list three types of employment that might arise on the coast near an offshore oilfield.

Feeder industries supply others: the tyre industry feeds the car industry. Other industries are offshoots: a fish canning industry may develop near fishing ports.

Industries develop to supply town populations with, for example, food, clothing, furniture and entertainment. These industries are often sited in or close to towns to keep transport costs low. Some industries are attracted to towns to take advantage of skilled workers there, of the many services provided and of good communications. Commercial services grow to service businesses, for example, insurance, warehousing and advertising.

As the standard of living in a community rises, so the demand for the service industries increases – for hairdressing, travel agents, estate agents, dry cleaners etc. Many industries expand with higher incomes: the sports industry, the news industry, the entertainment industry, the hotel industry etc. Whereas once manufacturing industry was the source of the wealth of the country, now most employment is provided by service industries.

So the reasons for the location of industry are varied, but the most common include the closeness to supplies of raw materials and skilled labour; the need for low transport costs, to be competitive; and for commercial services to be handy.

Q4 What is meant by a feeder industry? Think of and list three examples.

Q5 Think of and list three examples of offshoot industries.

Q6 Name five manufacturing industries that supply town populations.

Q7 Name ten service industries that supply town populations.

Q8 What are the most common reasons for the location of industry? Write a few sentences explaining or commenting on each, with examples.

Q9 Give three industries that exist in the town you live in, and the advantages there are for them.

Section 6

Specialisation

Just as people specialise in certain jobs, so do regions. In Britain, iron and steel trades developed in the Midlands with the presence of iron ore and coal workings. Sheffield became famous for cutlery and later the motor industry and allied industries developed in the area. Recently the computer industry has established itself to the West of London in what has become known as 'silicone valley'.

In the same way countries make the most of natural advantages, and specialise in those industries that they think can earn the most money. Spain, for example, has excellent beaches and months of sunshine: so it specialises in the tourist industry. Malaya specialised in rubber production because of her tropical rubber plantations.

The **specialisation** of certain regions in certain industries can be of great advantage to that area while those industries are booming. The pattern of production may shift however. New centres with more modern machinery and newer techniques may capture the market from older industries, as Japan and Korea have captured the shipbuilding industry from Britain and other European countries. New inventions such as man-made fibres may lead to the decline of older industries: the invention of synthetic rubber hit Malaya badly.

Developing countries may build their own manufacturing industries instead of exporting their raw materials for others to manufacture, as India has developed its cotton manufacturing industry. Low wage areas may undercut high wage countries, as Hong Kong has undercut the British clothing industry. The more specialised regions are the hardest hit if production patterns change. Not only may an industry close down but many other companies that serviced the industry, or its workers, may not be able to carry on.

If a country has few natural advantages it may choose to specialise in skilled workmanship, as Switzerland, with few raw materials and no coastline, specialised in watches and other high quality consumer goods. Britain has an experienced industrial population, though now suffering from shifts in the pattern of production. We no longer have a leading world place in cotton manufacture or shipbuilding or cars but the future may lie in high-technology industries that require skill but use few raw materials.

Q1 Why do certain regions or countries specialise in certain industries? Give two examples.

Q2 Give two disadvantages of regional specialisation.

Q3 Give three examples of industries in Britain that have declined with the shift of production advantage to other countries: and two examples of new industries which have developed in Britain.

Q4 How may a country with few natural advantages specialise? Give an example.

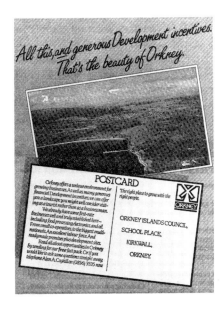

All this, and generous Development incentives.
That's the beauty of Orkney.

POSTCARD

Orkney offers a unique environment for growing businesses. As well as many generous financial Development incentives, we can offer you a landscape you might will consider visiting as a tourist rather than as a businessman.
We already have some first-rate businesses and truly established here—including food processing electronics and oil. From small co-operatives, to the biggest multi-nationals. An excellent labour force. And readymade premises plus development sites.
Read all about opportunities in Orkney by sending for our free fact pack. Or if you would like to ask some questions straight away telephone Alan A. Coghill on (0856) 3535 now.

The right place to grow with the right people.

ORKNEY ISLANDS COUNCIL,

SCHOOL PLACE,

KIRKWALL,

ORKNEY

Regional policy

In modern times less importance is attached to traditional reasons for industrial location. Energy supplies are available all over the country by pipeline or cable; transport costs have been reduced with the introduction of containers; and up-to-date information is instantly available by telecommunication and computer. Therefore many firms are "footloose" and are able to locate almost anywhere.

Employment opportunities are not evenly spread throughout the country. There is a concentration of jobs in the South-East near to London, the seat of government and the financial centre of the country, and to the continent. Different regions compete to attract new industries. Local authorities encourage firms to their localities by providing industrial sites or industrial estates, with good transport links, cheap rent and rates, or by relaxing building regulations to enable new factories to be built. Many governments have tried to encourage firms to areas of high unemployment by means of a **Regional Policy**. This may include tax allowances for investment in certain areas, or rent-free accommodation for the first few years. For a firm to consider moving to an area, not only is the **infra-structure** of road and rail links and housing etc. important, but also the local quality of life, with leisure and pleasure amenities.

Q5 Why are many firms "footloose" as regards location?

Q6 Give four reasons why there are more employment opportunities now in the South-East than in the North-West.

Q7 Why have governments introduced a regional policy?

Q8 Give three ways in which it is hoped to attract firms to areas of high unemployment.

Q10 Explain in your own words what is meant by the quality of life in an area.

Section 7

Chain of production

The different stages in the production and distribution of goods are linked by commercial services which are a necessary aid to widespread trade.

Study the diagram below, and answer the following questions

Q1 What is the product of the primary or extractive industry?
Q2 What is the product of the manufacturing industry?
Q3 Name the commodity market.
Q4 Give two types of transport used.
Q5 Give two stages of distribution after manufacture.
Q6 Name four stages at which the services of banks would be used, e.g. the coffee growers pay lorry owners to transport the crop to the port.
Q7 Name three risks against which insurance would be taken out in the chain.
Q8 At what stage do you think advertising would be most widely used?
Q9 Describe circumstances in which the coffee planter might himself become a consumer of the final product in this international chain of production.

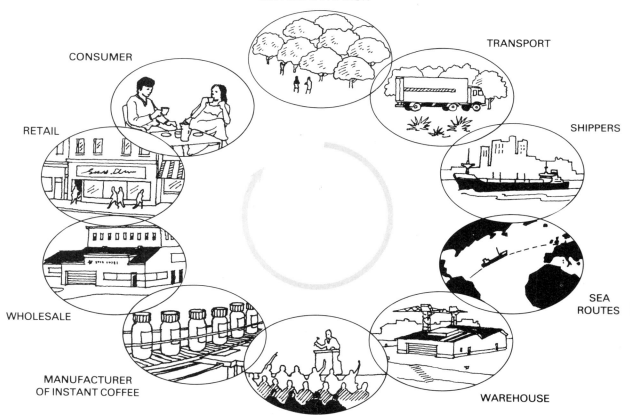

COFFEE PLANTATION

TRANSPORT

CONSUMER

SHIPPERS

RETAIL

SEA ROUTES

WHOLESALE

MANUFACTURER OF INSTANT COFFEE

COFFEE EXCHANGE

WAREHOUSE

Money-go-round

1 People earn wages, for producing goods and services.
2 Their wages are spent in shops etc, on goods and services.
3 Shops bank their profits.
4 Banks lend money to industries, to help them expand.
   Every worker is both a producer and a consumer. Money is circulated, i.e. passed from hand to hand.

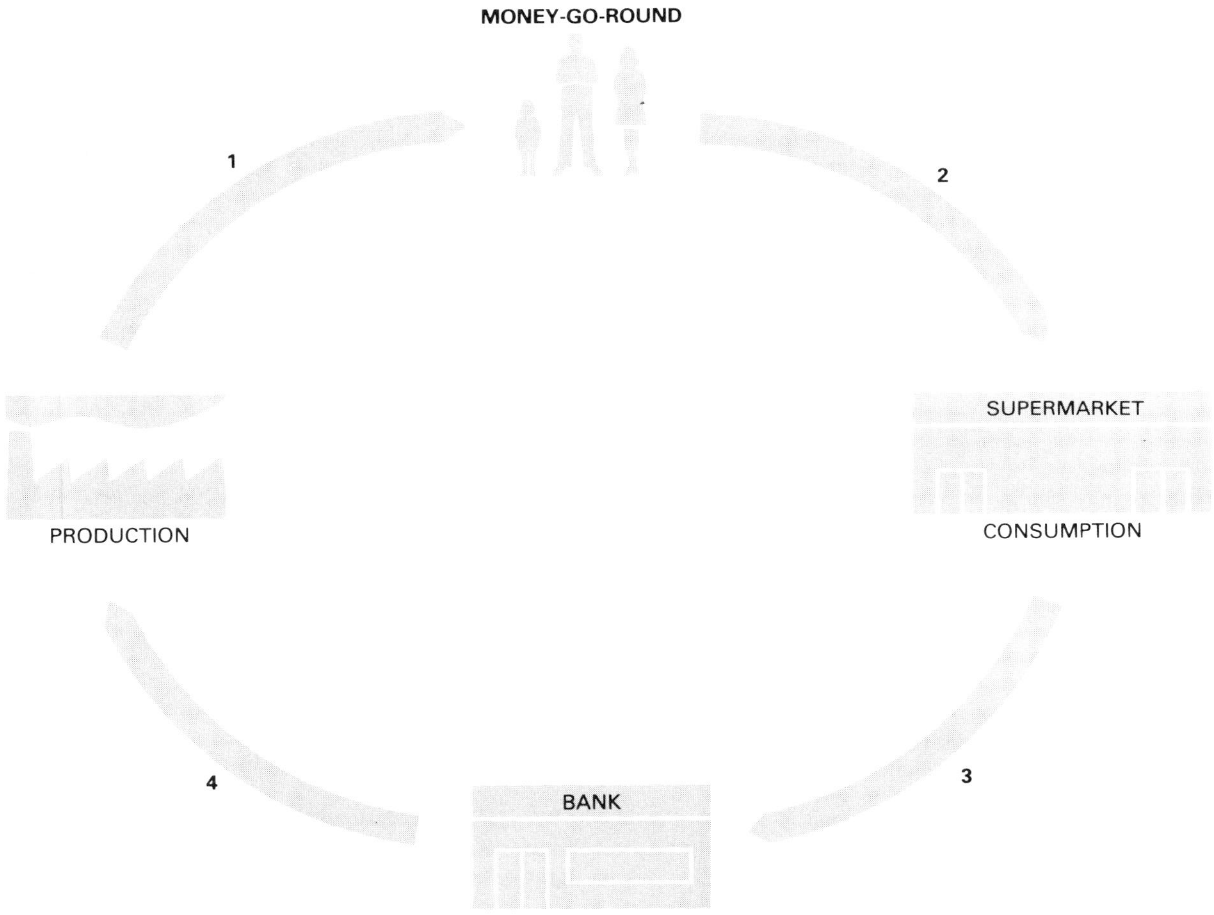

MONEY-GO-ROUND

1

2

PRODUCTION

SUPERMARKET

CONSUMPTION

4

3

BANK

Q1 Copy the diagram above, using half a page.
Q2 Put into your diagram more arrows, and letter each to show the flow of:
   a) family savings
   b) the banking of industries' profits
   c) personal loans to bank customers
   d) payments by shops for supplies received.

Section 8

Barter and money

Very primitive trade may be the exchanging or swopping of goods for other goods, e.g. a man with an extra axe may swop this for a blanket he needs. Exchanging goods for other goods is called **barter**. School children swopping marbles for sweets are bartering. Barter is still used in some societies.

The difficulties of barter do not allow for trade to develop widely. One man may not want what another is prepared to swop. Goods may not be easy to transport over a distance for barter.

What is needed for trade to develop is something that people are prepared to accept in exchange for anything, and that is light and easily carried or portable. Cowrie shells were widely used among primitive people as money, or a **medium of exchange**.

In many parts of the world a man's wealth was measured by his herds. The value of other goods was compared with that of a cow; this was the **measure of value**. However, a cow may be large or small, young or old, healthy or sick. Money can be used more exactly as a measure of value, to compare the price of one thing with that of another. A cow may die. Money should be longlasting or durable, and so a **store of value**.

Q1 What is barter?
Q2 Why is a system of barter not suitable for widespread trade?
Q3 Money has been called a) a medium of exchange
                               b) a measure of value
                               c) a store of value.
Write a sentence explaining each of these phrases.

Axe heads, beads, cattle, shells, metal pieces and many other things have been used as "money" at some time. Finally metal money proved most suitable. Gold and silver were scarce and hard to get: something too easily come by loses its value. When coins began to be minted under the King's control, of an equal or uniform shape, weight and pattern, their value could be relied upon and a great expansion of trade followed.

Coins could be made of different values, so change could be given, i.e. their values were divisible (they could be divided into parts).

Q4 The qualities necessary for a satisfactory "money" are listed below. Write a sentence explaining each. (Some of the words you will find on the previous page, and some above.)
a) portable   b) durable   c) uniform
d) acceptable e) scarce   f) divisible

Each country now has its own money or currency which is acceptable inside its frontiers, but not outside. The British currency is known as Sterling (£). If you travel to another country you must buy their currency to spend there, at the current rate of exchange, i.e. the price of one currency against another, e.g. $1.40 to £1. Banks deal in foreign exchange, i.e. buying and selling other currencies for Sterling.

Q5 What is the name of the British currency?
Q6 What are the currencies of
   a) France   b) USA
   c) Italy   d) Russia
   e) West Germany f) Spain
   g) Japan   h) India?
Q7 What is meant by foreign exchange?
Q8 What is meant by the rate of exchange?

Section 9

The development of Britain's trade

Steam power was invented in Britain in the 1700s, and developed to drive machinery. This led to the Industrial Revolution; and gave Britain a century's lead over other countries in the manufacture of cheap mass-produced goods. In the last century Britain was called the 'Workshop of the World'. Mass-produced goods were traded round the world; and the pattern of world sea routes showed shipping lanes radiating out from London and other British ports.

The pattern developed for British trade was the import of raw materials, and the export of finished goods. In this century, however, the traditional industries of coal, iron and steel, textiles and shipbuilding have declined. The coal industry has suffered from a switch to alternative fuels such as oil and gas; the iron and steel industry from low cost competition in the highly productive American and German foundries; the textile industry from cheap imports from the low-wage economies of the Far East; and shipbuilding from a fall in the world demand for ships, and strong foreign competition, especially from Japan.

Other countries have grown in industrial importance in the last fifty years, and now have a larger share of international trade than Britain. The USA, Germany, France and Japan have overtaken us in the output of mass-produced goods. Their industries are often more modern and efficient. The different countries of the Commonwealth have also grown stronger and independent. They now manufacture goods formerly imported from Britain. The growth in Britain's future trade seems towards the continent of Europe.

Britain has few raw materials, but a skilled industrial working class. She must specialise in producing goods that require highly skilled labour and sophisticated machinery. Therefore the new high technological industries e.g. home computers, telecommunications networks, are vital to her future. Britain developed commercial skills to aid its world trade—banking, insurance etc. These services have adapted and developed to changing world conditions: and London is still a world commercial centre.

Q1 Why was Britain called the "Workshop of the World"?
Q2 How has competition affected Britain's traditional industries?
Q3 List three goods that you or your family own which are foreign-made, and which you know are also made in this country.
Q4 Why is Britain a leading world country in commercial services?

The EEC

In 1978 Britain joined the **European Economic Community**, called the "Common Market". Members agreed to work towards the removal of the customs duties etc, of each separate country. Trade between member countries becomes "free"; but imported goods

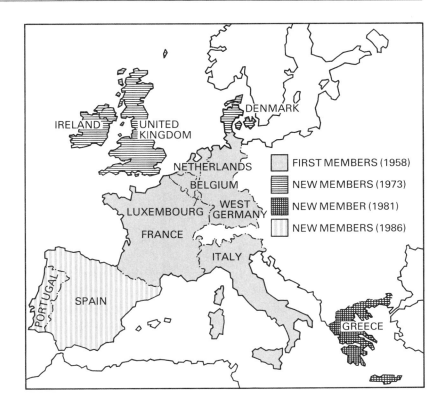

from the rest of the world are handicapped by tariffs (import duties). Another aim was to allow people to move freely within the Market, so that they could search for jobs; and to allow investment money to circulate freely so that firms could locate wherever they pleased.

The removal of restrictions inside the Market would allow greater division of labour, and larger production units, with greater output at lower cost turning out goods for the whole Market. This was necessary in order for Europe to compete with the other great trading blocks.

The Common Market is an enormous market of over 260 million people, compared with just over 200 million in the USA, and above 250 million in the USSR (Russia). There are other "common markets" in the world e.g. in the Caribbean; and they all aim to develop free trade between members, and to build a "common tariff wall" against the rest of the world, to protect home industries.

Q5 a) What trading block has Britain joined?
b) What is the size of its market?
c) Name the other countries concerned.
Q6 What are the advantages of having a larger common "market"?
Q7 What is it aimed to make "free" inside the EEC?
Q8 Explain what is meant by a "common tariff wall" against the rest of the world.

Section 10

Foreign trade

Britain is a densely populated island. To feed our population of 55 million, we **import** (buy from abroad) a quarter of the food we eat.

Also Britain has not enough raw materials to feed its many factories. We import wool, cotton, timber, rubber, minerals, oil and many other raw materials.

We also import semi-finished goods, such as unbleached cotton cloth; and we then put a finish on the product. Cloth may be bleached, dyed, printed, textured and made up into garments.

Goods imported from abroad have to be paid for in foreign currencies. We also pay for services abroad, e.g. holidays. To earn the foreign currencies necessary, we sell goods and services overseas, we **export**.

Britain is one of the industrial nations of the world exporting manufactured goods. This does not mean we do not also import manufactured goods, as you can see from the pie chart. UK companies like to order the best from anywhere in the world. Britain is also a world centre for commercial services and these earn foreign currencies, e.g. banking, insurance and shipping services. By selling our experienced commerical and industrial skills, we can afford the natural riches and products of other countries, e.g. tropical fruit and sunny holidays, in addition to buying basic food and raw materials.

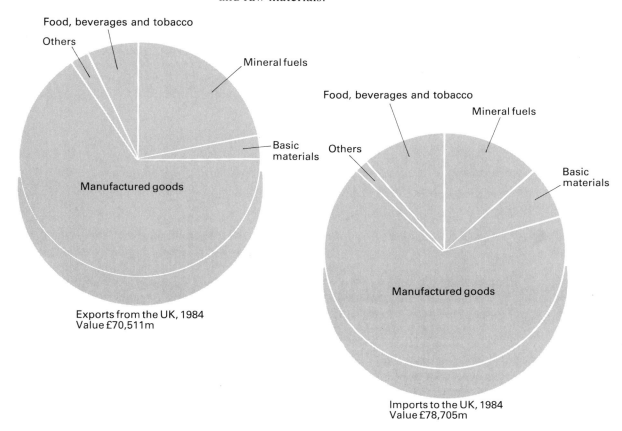

Food, beverages and tobacco
Others
Mineral fuels
Basic materials
Manufactured goods

Exports from the UK, 1984
Value £70,511m

Food, beverages and tobacco
Mineral fuels
Others
Basic materials
Manufactured goods

Imports to the UK, 1984
Value £78,705m

Q1 Why is Britain dependent on imports?

Q2 Think of five imported foods and list them with the countries they come from.

Q3 What raw materials are imported for our production of:

bread   winter coats

marmalade   towels

sweets   cigarettes

elastic   newspapers

Q4 What is meant by exports?

Q5 Give reasons why cars are both imported and exported.

Q6 Why are exports important for Britain?

Q7 Many countries earn foreign currencies by selling to others the riches of nature, in which they have a natural advantage. Give three examples which we buy.

Q8 How does Britain earn foreign currency?

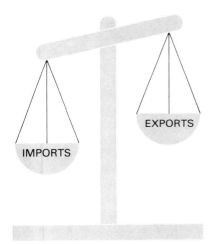

IMPORTS

EXPORTS

Balance of Trade

The decisions regarding buying and selling abroad are taken by individual companies. The total of imports and exports for the country as a whole are found from statistics collected, e.g. by HM Customs and Excise at our ports, published monthly and annually.

The comparison between the value of **goods** imported and exported in a year is called the **Balance of Trade**. Britain usually imports more goods than it exports. This gives an "unfavourable" or "adverse" Balance of Trade, because we are spending more than we are earning on goods and raw materials.

Balance of Payments

Payment is also received for **services** sold abroad, e.g. shipping services (cargo space on British boats and planes), banking and insurance services. These earners of foreign currencies are called **Invisible Exports**. We earn very much more for these services than we spend abroad on similar "invisible imports".

The total value of monies paid into and out of Britain in a year is set out in the **Balance of Payments**. These totals include payments for goods, payments for services, payments for embassies or soldiers overseas, grants and gifts etc. The balance is sometimes favourable and sometimes adverse.

Q9 What is the Balance of Trade?

Q10 What is meant by invisible exports?

Q11 What is the Balance of Payments? Give four examples of items included.

Q12 Is Britain's Balance of Trade usually favourable or adverse?

Q13 Name three invisible exports that help Britain's Balance of Payments.

Vocabulary

Assembly
Fitting together manufactured parts to make goods.

Automation
Production of goods where machines or robots do the work, controlled by computer, and a few workers keep a check on the process.

Balance of Payments
The comparison between the total money paid into and out of a country, involving foreign currency transactions, in a period (for example, a year).

Balance of Trade
The difference between the value of **goods** exported and imported in a given period, e.g. a year.

Barter
The direct exchange of goods and services for other goods and services.

Capital goods
Goods used again and again by businesses in order to carry out their trade, e.g. machinery, equipment, vehicles.

Commodity market
A world market for a crop or raw material.

Construction
Building roads, bridges, houses, etc.

Consumer goods
Goods bought and used by the general public.

Consumption
Goods and services used up, i.e. bought by the consumer.

Distribution
Transporting and trading, including wholesaling and retailing.

Division of labour
Specialisation in different jobs or processes.

Exchange
All arrangements for payment, i.e. money for goods.

Extractive
Drawn from the earth or sea. Extractive industries, also called **Primary** industries, are those producing food and raw materials.

Invisible exports
Earners of foreign currency that are "invisible" because no goods pass, i.e. services sold to foreign buyers.

Manufacture
Making goods from raw materials.

Market
Any getting together of buyers and sellers.

Mass-production
Manufacture on a large scale, of identical goods, using powered machinery.

Mechanisation
The mass-production of goods by machinery which the worker operates.

Production
Goods or services for which people pay.

Primary Production
Production that comes first (primary), i.e. of raw materials.

Service industries
Services sold widely to the general public

Specialisation
Concentration of a person on one trade, process or skill; or of a region or country on one product.

Wholesale markets
Markets supplying perishables to the trade.

2 Retailing

We can buy in all kinds of ways — in shops, from mail order catalogues, from machines, on the doorstep, by letter or by telephone! All these types of retailing compete with each other, suiting different people at different times. They compete by price, quality or services offered. We are all experienced shoppers used to shopping, comparing and selecting our purchases from a wide range of goods offered. We also buy a variety of services, e.g. entertainment, travel, sport. In this chapter we tell you something of how these different types of retailing are organised.

Sections
1. The Function of the Retailer   Unit Shops
   A Case Study: What should they do?
2. Multiples
3. Supermarkets   Hypermarkets
4. The Franchise Retail Outlet
5. The Department Store
6. Mail Order   Postal Sales
7. Automatic Vending   Discount Stores
8. Door-to-door Sales
9. Selling Parties   Mobile Shops   Open Air Markets

Section 1

The Function of the Retailer

The retailer sells goods in small quantities to the consumer. The function of the retailer is to have the right goods, at the right time and at the right price to suit his customers. Most retailing is done through shops. Shops can be large or small; sell one type of goods or a variety of products; be independent or one of a series of shops selling the same range and owned by the same firm, i.e. a chain store.

Unit Shops

Unit Shops are independent shops. Most are small.

The little store in the picture below might be in the outback of Australia and the only shop of a small community of farmers.

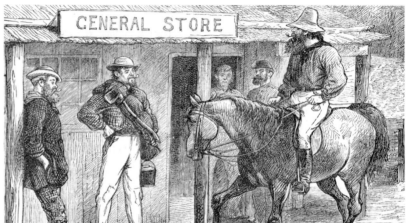

Q1 Under each of these headings, list three lines of goods the store might stock:

groceries	paints and oils	clothing
hardware	dry goods	boots and shoes

Q2 A village in Britain often has a "general store" selling a variety of goods.
   a) Why do you think this is?
   b) Write a description of a village shop you have seen.

In towns, a far greater variety of shops is found. Small shops generally specialise in certain kinds of goods or services. Many are owned by one person.

Q3 Give four types of unit shop you would expect to find in a town.

Q4 What can a unit shop do to compete with larger shops offering cheaper prices or a greater variety of goods?

Q5 Why do some people prefer to give their custom to small local shops?

Q6 What do you think would be a good location for a small shop selling sweets, ices and newspapers?

Q7 Give two examples of unit shops selling services rather than goods.

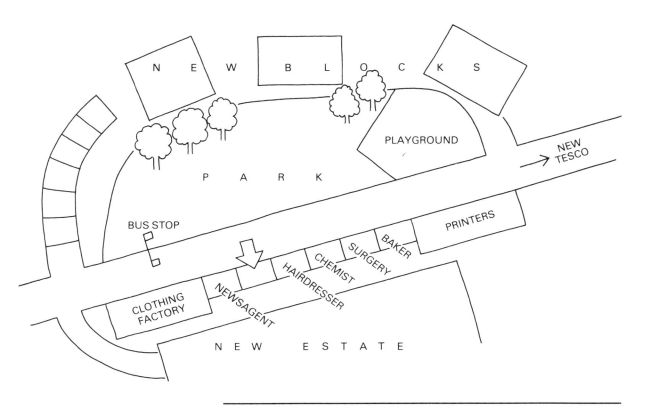

A Case Study: What Should They do?

Bert Lovejoy and his wife Ethel have owned and run a general provisions store for many years in the outskirts of Liverpool. Up to now they have made a reasonable living, opening the shop from 9.00 a.m. to 5.30 p.m.

The surrounding population has gradually changed, as slums have been pulled down and new blocks of flats built. Over the last year there has been a large increase in population as a number of new building projects have been completed. Now there is enough potential business to attract a supermarket; and a Tesco Supermarket is being built a mile away on the bus route to Liverpool.

The Lovejoys' is a general provisions counter store. You can buy a loaf of bread, potatoes, some German sausage, a mop and a packet of screws! Bert has the habit of buying a crate of any item a customer has asked for that is not in stock. But his particular interest is in delicatessen — continental cheeses, pâtè, cooked meats, etc. Ethel's interests are different; she enjoys going to the wholesale market early in the morning and buying the greengrocery for the shop. They have always kept customer services to a minimum, not giving any credit for example.

Q8 Can they survive the new competition? Should they pack up and set up business elsewhere? Should they change the style of shop? Study the map carefully and write about what you would advise them to do, giving your reasons.

Section 2

Multiples

When a shop is part of a chain of more than 10 shops under one firm, it is called a multiple. Each shop or branch has a manager, but the buying is done centrally; and the range of goods and services, the pricing policy, and the look of the shops are decided at the head office.

Many multiples specialise mainly in one type of goods e.g. Dolcis. These are called **specialist chains**. Others are well-known for stocking a great variety of goods e.g. Marks and Spencer; these are called **variety chains**.

Q1 Give the names of specialist chains in
   a) furniture
   b) shoes
   c) electrical goods
   d) men's tailoring
   e) women's clothes
   f) groceries
   g) toiletries
   h) dry cleaning
   i) stationery

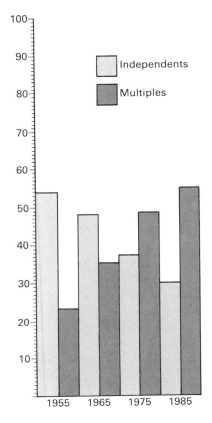

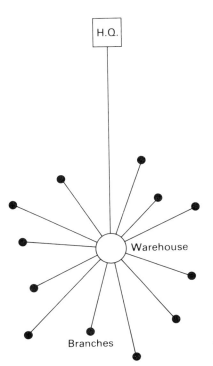

Q2 Give the names of three variety chains.

Q3 How would you recognise a shop belonging to a multiple you know, in a strange town,
a) from the outside
b) inside?

Q4 List three of the duties that fall on the manager of a branch of a multiple.

Q5 Listed below are some of the many aspects of a large retail multiple. Copy the list, and mark each item H (Head Office) or B (Branch) according to which you think would be responsible.
a) advertising
b) shop design
c) shelf stacking
d) cheap lines
e) shop assistants
f) wages
g) banking the takings
h) new sites for expansion
i) replacement stock ordering.

Q6 Look at the chart. What is the percentage of the market held by independent shops compared with multiples in 1955, 1965, 1975 and 1985?

The High Street has become increasingly dominated by "giants", the large multiples. The small independent shop cannot survive with such competition nearby.

Orders for standard stock items in all multiple branches can be bulked, and very large orders placed direct with manufacturers, thus cutting out the wholesaler or "middleman". A **bulk discount** is obtained and this advantage can be used to cut prices and capture customers. A multiple may set up its own warehouses to supply branches. Organisation can be streamlined across branches, e.g. for advertising, stock control, wages calculation. There is enough capital in the business to modernise shops, to employ retailing experts and to expand into new areas.

Q7 Copy the diagram.

Q8 What advantages has a multiple to enable it to capture customers?

Many multiples are now so large that they are known countrywide. The size of shops and the variety of goods stocked are growing steadily.

Q9 What is the main appeal to the customer of a multiple?

Some multiples, such as Marks and Spencer and Littlewoods, order goods from manufacturers to their own design and under their own brand. Some multiples, for example shoe or chemist chains, are linked to manufacturing.

Q10 Give the name of three own-brands in variety chain stores.

27

Section 3

Supermarkets

Supermarkets are large shops centring on grocery sales, but including a wide variety of food and drink sales, as well as other everyday goods. A supermarket is nearly always owned by a grocery chain.

Supermarkets use most of the following methods to raise sales. Often the customer is not aware of them.

1. A display of plenty encourages you to take more.
2. Every day items like sugar are placed low to make the shopper look down all the shelves to reach them.
3. At eye-level luxury, high-profit goods tempt the shopper to impulse buying. The retailer often makes large profits on these items.
4. A loudspeaker may lull the shopper with soft music, or suggest purchases as "recipes of the day".
5. The shop is arranged to make the shopper walk past all the shelves.
6. Sweets and goods to tempt children are placed low to catch their eyes and near check-out points where they will be queueing.
7. Some cut prices are specially advertised in the windows to draw customers into the shop. These goods may even be sold below cost price at a loss and are called **loss leaders**. Once the shopper is in the supermarket other items will be purchased; and extra pence may be added to other prices.

Q1 What is a "loss leader"?

Q2 Give five examples of every day items you might purchase in a supermarket and five examples of luxuries you might be tempted to buy.

Q3 What do you think impulse buying is?

Q4 Draw a floor plan of a supermarket you know and label the main selling areas.

Quiz

		Score
Q1	What is the main type of goods sold by supermarkets?	1
Q2	Name three types of food sold separately in small specialist shops which are brought together in a supermarket.	3
Q3	Give three ways in which goods are displayed.	3
Q4	How does the shopper collect the goods in a supermarket?	1
Q5	Who does the shopper pay for the goods?	1
Q6	Which of the following attractions draw customers to a supermarket? a) delivery b) credit c) cut prices d) help and advice from shop assistants e) one-stop shopping f) wide selection g) take-your-own-time h) Sunday opening	4
Q7	Give four non-food types of goods sold in supermarkets.	4
Q8	Are supermarkets branches of well-known grocery chains?	1
Q9	Are supermarkets tending to get larger or smaller?	1
Q10	Is the range of goods being increased in supermarkets?	1
Q11	Are the chains' own brands of groceries cheaper than manufacturers' brands?	1
Q12	Give two items which are often sold by counter service in a supermarket?	2
Q13	Where are sweets displayed and why?	2
	Total possible score	25

Hypermarkets

These are great out-of-town supermarkets designed for the car-owning weekly shopper. The enormous sales floor centres round the sale of food; but also displays many other goods including hardware, clothes, kitchen equipment. It may include a cafe and other services. The shopper wheels a trolley out to the car park surrounding the hypermarket.

Section 4

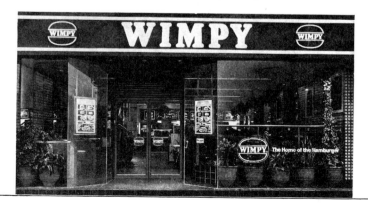

The franchise retail outlet

Many shops trading under the same name are not multiples, but franchise businesses. The owners hold a "franchise" or licence to sell those goods or services using someone else's well-known name. Franchise businesses include Wimpy bars, the Body Shops (toilet preparations), Dyno-Rod (drain cleaning), Prontoprint (duplicating), British School of Motoring, and Hertz Rent-a-Car. Other franchise retail outlets are in carpet cleaning, weed control and car repairs etc. The list of franchise businesses grows yearly.

A franchise is bought by a hopeful trader from a Franchise Company who, in return for a lump sum, supplies the equipment and trains the new trader (franchisee) on how to run the business. The Franchise Company has all the experience and know-how necessary and wants to expand sales, not by opening new branches itself, but by selling franchises to people who are eager to work hard in their own business. Often the Franchise Company selects a suitable site where the new franchisee has a good chance of success; and arranges for credit or loan facilities.

The new trader signs a contract that she will get her equipment and continue to order her supplies from the Franchise Company, and that she will pay a continuing royalty for the franchise. This royalty is usually based on the total sales in a period e.g. 10% of total sales per quarter. The franchisee remains her own boss and owner of the business but uses the well-known name and distinctive sign of the Franchise Company.

Wimpy are launching a number of these new counter service outlets at prime locations in your area.

We're offering each of them, on a franchise basis, to individuals or companies who are looking to invest £150,000 or more.

Although, essentially, you'll be running your own business, as a Wimpy franchisee you'll have plenty of security behind you. We're the biggest franchisers in the U.K., operating in the catering business for over 25 years. And backed by United Biscuits – a successful multi-million group.

Your outlet would be planned by us with the very latest decor and machinery. You'd have total support in terms of marketing, advertising, product, sales and service.

We'll train you and your staff and offer advice and ideas on, amongst other things, how to increase traffic into your Wimpy.

We'd like to stress that a franchise works both ways however. And we demand total involvement from whoever joins us. So, if hard work has never agreed with you it's highly unlikely you'll ever agree with us.

Nevertheless, the rewards are high and within your grasp.

Ring us. You won't lose anything by picking up the 'phone. You might lose a great deal if you don't.

(Example. 1981)

Q1 By using the following headings, make notes of what a franchise business is and how it is formed.
a) lump sum payment
b) training
c) contract
d) royalty.

Q2 Who owns a new franchise business?

Q3 What do all franchised businesses of one Franchise Company have in common? Give examples from a franchise business you are familiar with.

Q4 Read the 1981 Wimpy advertisement opposite. What services are being offered by the Franchise Company in exchange for a lump sum payment?

The franchise business is becoming very popular, with 350 companies offering different franchises in Britain. Franchises can be bought for as little as £8,000 and as much as £1,000,000. They carry advantages for the customer as well as for the Company and the franchisee.

The consumer enjoys the supply of a product which he knows is of a consistent standard and is widely available. A Wimpy bar in London will sell the same basic food and drink as a Wimpy bar in Manchester. Both bars will look similar so that they can be easily recognised.

The Franchise Company is able to expand at a much faster rate than if it had to find all the money for the new "outlets". Furthermore, it does not have the trouble of running or staffing these outlets.

Finally, from the point of view of the new franchisee, she is going into business to sell a product which has already been tested and proved successful. She also has the backing of a big organisation who arrange national advertising as well as new product research; and often keeps a check on all franchise holders to make sure they keep to the high standards set down. Yet she is still her own boss, working hard for her own business. New franchise businesses are more likely to succeed than other new businesses, with the independent trader's energy backed by large-scale expertise.

Q5 What advantage is gained by consumers from franchise businesses?

Q6 What advantage is gained from a franchise contract by the Franchise Company?

Q7 Give three advantages gained from a franchise contract by a new franchisee.

Q8 Why do some Franchise Companies keep a regular check on franchise holders?

Q9 'Little Chef'', "Hertz Rent-a-Car" and "Prontoprint" are examples of franchise businesses. What do you think makes these businesses especially suitable for a franchise?

Section 5

The department store

Department stores have been called "one-stop shopping". All types of goods are sold in different departments on many floors. Department stores have well-known names. Many are, in fact, part of large groups.

Q1 Mrs Baker and her daughter Teresa, who is shortly to move into her first unfurnished flat, plan a day's shopping in the department store. They arrive at 10 a.m. and leave at 5 p.m. Plan their day, hour by hour.

Q2 a) List the goods on the ground floor.
b) How are these displayed?
c) Why do you think they are placed between the doors and the lifts?

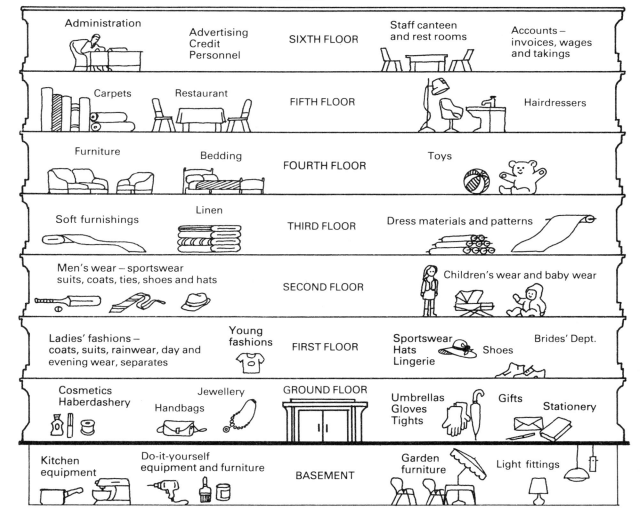

Q3 Other floors are divided into separate departments.
a) What departments are on the first floor?
b) What is the link between them?

Q4 Why are the furniture department, the restaurant and the hairdressers generally on the top floors of stores?

Q5 What are the advantages of shopping for clothes in a department store compared with a variety chain?

Q6 List the surroundings and services that make shopping comfortable or luxurious.

Q7 The manager of a department is often called the Buyer. Why?

Q8 List all the Buyers' responsibilities in a department.

Q9 Why is the job of a Buyer in a department with six staff more important than that of a branch manager of a clothing chain, with the same number of staff?

1 THE BUYER SELECTS AND ORDERS ALL THE GOODS IN THE DEPARTMENT

2 SHE ARRANGES THE DISPLAYS IN THE DEPARTMENT

3 SHE DECIDES ON WHICH GOODS TO ADVERTISE (WITH THE ADVERTISING DEPT.)

4 THE BUYER FIXES THE PRICES OF GOODS

5 SHE TRAINS AND MANAGES THE DEPARTMENT'S SALES STAFF

6 SHE ORGANISES THE SALES IN HER DEPARTMENT

Q10 When and why are Sales held?

Q11 List the central offices serving all the departments in the store, and write sentences saying what you think is the work of each.

Q12 What services to the customer are offered in a department store which are not generally offered in variety chains?

Q13 Department stores have been called one-stop shopping, and so have supermarkets. Supermarkets centre on weekly food sales. What are the main types of goods sold in Department stores?

Q14 Department stores make a special feature of their window displays in contrast to variety chains. Describe an attractive window display you have seen.

Section 6

Mail order

Quiz

		Score
Q1	How are mail order goods displayed?	1
Q2	How are the goods ordered and how are they supplied?	2
Q3	Describe how payment is made for the goods.	2
Q4	What benefits are received by the agent of a mail order company?	2
Q5	What type of persons are typically agents?	2
Q6	Mention two kinds of people who would appreciate home shopping.	2
Q7	Select the correct alternative in the lines below. Catalogues	
	a) are black and white/multi-coloured	
	b) include only clothes/a wide variety of goods	
	c) include well-known manufacturers' brands/unbranded goods/own-brands/a variety of these.	
	d) are issued once a year/several times a year.	4
Q8	What action should you take if you are not satisfied with goods?	2
Q9	Give two jobs done by agents.	2
Q10	What records are kept by agents ?	2
Q11	Give three advantages of fireside shopping.	3
Q12	If payment is 5p per week for every £1 spent, how many weeks' credit is given?	
Q13	Give three possible dangers with mail order buying.	3
Q14	Why do you think that mail order has grown so fast in recent years?	1
Q15	In what type of goods do mail order do the bulk of their business?	1

Total possible score 30

A mail order warehouse

Mail Order Organisation
Mail order businesses need
a) a large space for the storage of goods
b) sufficient money to tide them over while instalment payments are made by customers
c) catalogues to advertise their stock.

Two main groups dominate the mail order market — Littlewoods and Great Universal Stores. Each issues several catalogues under different names. Usually, they are in colour, advertising some 20,000 different items and are issued twice a year.

The warehouse above is situated beside the railway and overhead carriers convey the addressed parcels direct to the station for despatch. Orders are received at the warehouse, checked and packed; and accounts are kept for each agent and each customer.

Q1 What is needed by a mail order business?
Q2 In two columns compare the expenses of
   a) a mail order business
   b) a retail chain.

Postal Sales

Postal sales is the name given for goods ordered from newspaper and magazine advertisements. "Payment with order" is the general rule. By advertising, manufacturers or wholesalers can reach the consumer direct.

Q3 What are postal sales? Give examples of five goods commonly sold in this way.
Q4 What do mail order and postal sales have in common? Give two ways in which they are different.

Section 7

Automatic vending

This is the sale of food, drink and other suitable goods from automatic slot machines.

Q1 Sandra (below) uses several slot machines during the day. What might they be?

Q2 List two items each for goods sold by machine
   a) food and drink
   b) other?

Q3 Give two advantages of automatic shopping.

Q4 Give two disadvantages of automatic shopping.

Q5 Some companies rent sites for their automatic machines and keep them stocked up by van. Give two sites which might be suitable.

Mr Black of Super Machine Catering and Vending Company calls on the manager of Crossman and White's Ltd.

Q7 List the advantages claimed by the representative above for automatic meals machines.

Q8 What are the advantages of drinks machines in offices or factories?

Discount Stores

Discount stores sell mainly hardware that can be selected by brand name. Their main attraction is the low prices offered. They save on costs by bulk buying for their branches, and keeping shop display and service to a minimum. Shopping there is like buying from warehouses. However, credit terms and delivery may be provided.

Q9 How do discount stores manage to cut prices below other shops?

Section 8

Door-to-door sales

"Good morning madam. I'm from the Education Department. I've come to discuss your children's education. How old are they? . . . . Have you seen these children's encyclopedias? They are beautifully produced with pictures and very educational, and will be a great help with homework. You can buy the set for only £1 a week."

BEWARE! Mum thinks the caller is from the County Education Department, but he only represents his company's education department.

BEWARE! The representative gains the confidence and interest of the housewife before he admits he is there to sell.

BEWARE! Consider whether the total price is reasonable before thinking whether you can afford the instalments.

Mrs Smith was attracted by a leaflet advertising low-priced carpets with a special offer of free laying. The representative called with samples; she chose her colours and the company came and laid her fitted carpet. She was delighted! — but not for long. A year later the carpet was already worn bare in patches. She looked up the address of the company to complain to them, but could make no contact. They had vanished.

BEWARE! The fly-by-night firm, selling poor quality goods.

"Good morning! I'm from the Speedy Sew Machine Company. You filled out a coupon for our bargain mini machine. May I come in? I'm afraid I've only got the demonstration model with me but I'll show you that. Unfortunately there's a six weeks' delay in supply. Of course you can't expect too much of these little machines at this price. I shouldn't really be saying this, but frankly, madam, I think you are wasting your money. Compare it with this other machine I've got here. Look at what this one can do! Granted, it is a bit dearer; but it will last for years — and what a difference to your home dressmaking! I'll tell you what I'll do, as a favour. I'll leave it here for you to try out for a couple of weeks without obligation."

BEWARE! 'Switch-selling', advertises bargains, with every intention of selling you another, dearer article.

BEWARE! Once you've tried something out you may not want to part with it, even if it costs more than you wanted to pay.

"I'm afraid I don't think any of these photographs are very good of the children."

"Well, madam, decide what you want, and I'll take the order."

"I don't really want any."

"You can't say that. I've wasted my time coming up here to take the photographs and then coming back to show you the proofs. That's cost me money and time. I can't make a living like that. It's not good enough. You've got to order now."

"Don't try to bully me, please. You came to the door offering to take photographs in the home without obligation. That means that I didn't agree to buy anything, and I don't want to order now. You took the risk, and I'm afraid in this case it has not come off. Goodbye."

BEWARE! Don't let salesmen bully you. Don't buy anything you don't really want, at the price.

Don't buy because you feel sorry for the salesman.

Q1 Read the case studies above and summarise in your own words four methods of selling to beware of.

Q2 Many door-to-door sales are genuine value for money. Give two advantages to the housewife.

Q3 What information should you get from the doorstep salesman?

Q4 Why might you be wiser to go down to a shopping centre for the goods you want?

Q5 Give three examples of goods sold door-to-door.

Section 9

Selling parties

A housewife may volunteer to invite friends and neighbours to a tea party at which a certain firm's products are on display, e.g. jewellery. The hostess receives a payment towards the food provided, a commission on sales and a present from the firm. The guests are expected to order the goods.

Q1 Give two examples of goods sold through parties.
Q2 In two columns give
  a) the advantages,
  b) the disadvantages, to
  i) the hostess;   ii) the firm;   iii) the guests.

Mobile shops

A mobile shop is any travelling selling point of goods and services.

Q3 Give three types of mobile or travelling shop.
Q4 What are the advantages of this type of shop?
Q5 Give three sets of people who might particularly welcome a mobile shop.

Open air markets

Q6 Give six types of goods sold at markets.
Q7 Write a description of a market you know, either a country market or a street market. State
  a) how it is arranged
  b) when it is held
  c) how some stallowners attract customers
  d) the variety of goods sold
  e) the atmosphere
Q8 Markets continue to attract crowds even in busy shopping centres. What are three attractions of markets?
Q9 Why are market goods cheaper than shops'?

A market involves the local council in many arrangements, e.g. the site, street cleaning, traffic control. Markets may only be held in accordance with local council regulations. Some sites are very old, having been used as markets for centuries; some are new; some are traditionally held in certain streets and on certain days. The council may appoint a market Superintendent who allocates and rents out sites for stalls.

Any stallholder selling goods off the market site has to be separately licensed as a street trader.

Q10 What steps does the local council take in connection with markets?

Q11 Imagine the day, from dawn to dusk, of a vegetable stall-holder in a market and write about it.

Q12 Certain pavement-sellers always keep an eye open for the police. Why is this?

Q13 What goods are often sold by pavement traders?

Q14 Draw a plan of any market site you know well, showing traffic flows, arrangement of stalls and the goods sold.

Vocabulary

Automatic vending
Machine sales.

Brand
The easily recognisable name under which a product or a range of goods or services is marketed.

Department store
A very large store on several floors divided into many departments each under its own buyer.

Discount stores
Goods sold at low cost direct from a warehouse with little sales assistance.

Hypermarkets
Great out-of-town supermarkets designed for the car-owning weekly shopper, with large parking

Loss leaders
Goods sold by a retailer at a loss in order to attract custom.

Mail order
Shopping from catalogues, sometimes through agents, and using credit.

Multiple
A chain of 10 or more branch shops under the same ownership. Each branch has the same name, style, and range of goods and prices.

Postal sales
Goods ordered from newspaper and magazine advertisements. Payment with order is generally required.

Representative
A travelling salesperson visiting retailers or potential customers.

Retailing
To sell in small quantities.

Specialist chains
Multiples specialising in one main type of goods, e.g. groceries or shoes.

Supermarket
Very large grocery store selling by self-service, not only groceries, but other food and drink (meat, vegetables etc) and other everyday goods such as clothing, household items.

Unit shops
These are single shops owned by one person, partners or a company.

Variety chains
Multiples known for the wide variety they stock, e.g. Woolworth, Marks and Spencer.

3 Wholesaling

Retailers will want to see a variety of manufacturers' products, to choose their stock by the style, quality and price suitable for their customers. The wholesaler traditionally provides this service for retailers in an area. Wholesalers buy in bulk from manufacturers, and store the goods in warehouses, so that they are quickly available to retailers.

Sections

Section 1

Order of distribution

The Wholesaler traditionally plays a part in the distribution of goods between the manufacturer and the retailer.

The Wholesaler buys in large quantities from a number of manufacturers enabling the retailer to have a choice of quality and price.

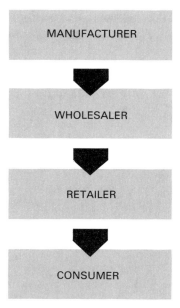

MANUFACTURER

WHOLESALER

RETAILER

CONSUMER

Q1 What is the traditional "Order of Distribution"?

Q2 Copy the diagram below showing the pattern of wholesale distribution.

Q3 Why do you think that the manufacturer prefers to sell to the wholesaler rather than to retail shops?

Q4 Why do you think a retailer might prefer to buy from a wholesaler instead of direct from a manufacturer?

Q5 Explain how there is a decrease, at each stage of distribution, as regards a) the area covered by sales
b) the size of each sale (see page 7).

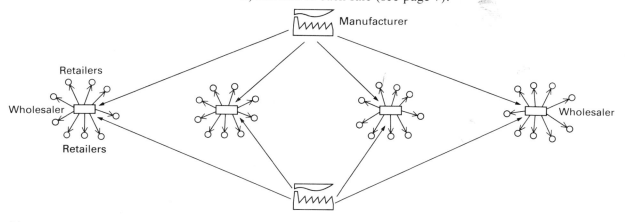

The function of the wholesaler

The wholesaler gives useful service to both manufacturer and retailer. The manufacturer wants to concentrate on his production lines, and not have to worry about distribution and marketing. The wholesaler buys in bulk and thus helps to lessen the problem of whether the manufacturer will sell sufficient items to cover the production costs. The larger the order at one time, the more the manufacturer is pleased: so a quantity deduction, a **bulk discount**, is allowed.

The wholesaler's main function is to store goods in quantity. They are then available for the retailer, who can choose between different manufacturers' products. The retailer takes smaller quantities because of limited stock room, and wishes to display as varied a stock as possible. A steady supply of deliveries from the wholesaler helps to steady prices in the shops, and prevents prices rising because of shortages. Retailers expect a period of credit from the wholesaler to give them time to sell the goods. To encourage early payment the wholesaler offers a **cash discount** (e.g. 3 per cent off for payment within a month).

The wholesaler gives news of new products to the retailer; and information to the manufacturer about how different lines are selling.

Q6 What advantage does the manufacturer get from the wholesaler?

Q7 What advantage does the retailer get from the wholesaler?

Q8 What is the main function of the wholesaler?

Q9 What would happen to the price of boots in a snowy winter if retailers could not get enough supplies? How does the wholesaler help to steady prices?

Q10 Write a paragraph explaining how the price of goods increases at each level of distribution.

Q11 Some say that goods could be cheaper without the "middleman" making a profit. Discuss what jobs done by the wholesaler would then have to be done at other levels.

Value added at each stage

MANUFACTURER

WHOLESALER

RETAILER

CONSUMER

Cost price

Handling costs

Profit

Section 2

Organisation of a wholesale business

1 The wholesaler buys in bulk; so his **Buyer** must use great judgement in ordering from different manufacturers, as mistakes might be costly!

2 The manufacturer delivers the bulk orders which are checked in on receipt.

3 The **Warehouse**, where the goods are stored, is the centre of the wholesale business.

4 The **Display** area shows samples of the goods in stock for retailers to see.

5 The wholesaler cannot rely on retailers visiting him to see goods and place orders. **Representatives**, or **travellers**, go out to visit retailers with catalogues, price lists and **order forms**. They may also carry samples. They pass on news of new lines etc. and receive information on how different lines are selling.

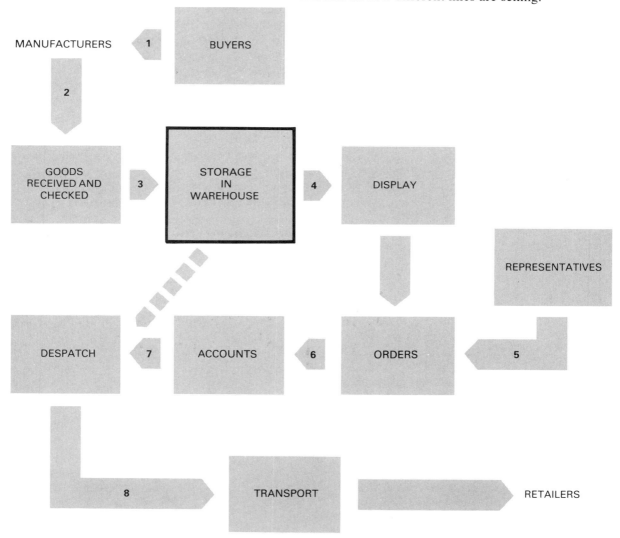

6 The retailers will want a chance to sell the goods before making payment and a period of credit is normally allowed by the wholesaler. However, a limit to the amount owing on credit may be fixed for each customer. Very careful accounts must be kept by the **Accounts** Department of amounts owing and paid by each retailer customer. To encourage them not to delay payment, a **cash discount** is allowed for settlement within a month. A **trade** or **quantity discount**, which increases with the amount of goods ordered, encourages retailers to place large orders.

7 After the order has been agreed and recorded by the Accounts Department, the goods are assembled and packed in the **Despatch** Department and passed on to the **Transport** section for delivery.

Q1 Copy and label the diagram "Organisation of a Wholesale Business".

Q2 Why has a wholesale buyer such an important job?

Q3 What are the two ways in which wholesalers obtain orders from retailers?

Q4 Why is the Accounts Department so important?

Q5 What is meant by trade discount?

Q6 How does the wholesaler encourage customers to settle quickly?

Q7 What is the job of a representative?

Q8 What does the inside of a warehouse look like?

Q9 Look at the diagram, and the photograph above. What do you think is the job of a warehouse worker?

Section 3

The wholesalers' problems

The High Street is increasingly dominated by giant retailers who handle enormous quantities of goods for their many shops. These "giants" can order in bulk direct from manufacturers, thus getting the advantage of bulk discounts themselves, while doing away with the wholesaler's profit. These giant retailers now supply half the goods bought by the public. Less than a third of retail sales now remain in the hands of small shops, who obtain supplies from wholesalers.

The number of customers supplied by wholesalers has therefore fallen considerably. They also suffer increasingly from other difficulties. Large warehouse premises in town centres are hard to find and expensive, while traffic jams and parking problems make delivery to shops more difficult. If the warehouse is moved to a cheaper country site, delivery distances are increased. Many wholesalers have gone out of business. Others have survived by reorganising their type of business.

Q1 Give three growing difficulties of a wholesaler.

Q2 Explain whether the wholesaler can solve these difficulties by moving out of town.

Q3 Who are a wholesaler's customers? Why has the number of these customers decreased over recent years?

Q4 Give two examples of how giant retailers capture customers from smaller shops.

Q5 Why are goods bought by the small retailer more expensive than supplies bought by the giant retailer?

Cash and carry wholesaling

Some wholesalers have succeeded on a Cash and Carry basis. They enable retailers to buy goods as cheaply as possible by cutting out all services, such as credit and transport. At the warehouse the

range of goods is displayed as at a supermarket, but with the stock number against each item. Only "trade" customers are allowed, i.e. retailers. Each completes an order form with the quantity of each stock item required, pays on the spot and carries away the cartons in his or her own car.

Q6 What advantage does the retailer gain from buying stocks from a Cash and Carry warehouse?

Q7 In order to get this advantage, what wholesale services does the retailer have to do without?

Direct selling

Some wholesalers may try to sell goods direct to the consumer with newspaper advertisements.

Q8 Do you think that goods sold direct from a warehouse are likely to be cheaper than those in shops? If so why?

Section 4

Voluntary groups and chains

How can small retailers keep their independence and yet gain the advantages of bulk buying, and so compete with the bigger organisations?

The answer: to get together in a **voluntary group** to do their own wholesaling. Send all the orders in together to the manufacturer and claim the bulk discount.

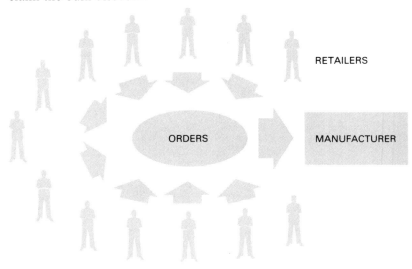

How can the wholesaler make sure that he keeps a good regular round of retail customers, and so survive?

The answer: a **voluntary chain**. Agreement is reached with a number of retailers to link themselves with a group of wholesalers. The retailers agree to buy a regular amount of goods from them, in return for cut prices and other benefits and help. The wholesaler can then be sure of a large block order; and can organise his visits and deliveries.

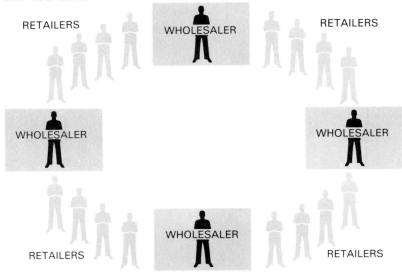

Voluntary Groups and Chains have been so successful that some are now amongst the largest wholesale/retail organisations in the country. The wholesalers order from manufacturers in this country and on the Continent. They advertise widely their own group brand names. They give retail members the benefit of expert advice on display, shop layout, accounting etc. They offer cheap insurance, and cut-price products.

The voluntary groups and chains have helped independents to survive. They aim to combine the personal, friendly service of the local family shop and the keenness of the independent owner, with the benefits and competitive prices of the larger organisation.

Q1 What is a voluntary group?

Q2 Copy the diagram illustrating a voluntary chain.

Q3 What is a voluntary chain?

Q4 What are the advantages to the wholesaler in a voluntary chain?

Q5 What are the advantages to the retailer in a voluntary chain?

Q6 What are the advantages to the consumer in buying at a shop belonging to a voluntary group or chain?

Q7 From the illustrations below give the names of voluntary groups and chains, two selling groceries and one other.

Section 5

Produce or wholesale markets

Perishable goods cannot be stored for any length of time in warehouses, but must be restocked daily. The wholesalers who deal in perishables work in **Produce** or **Wholesale markets**, organised for vast deliveries from the countryside and abroad every 24 hours. Supplies are coming in to London and other big towns all through the night: and retailers, buyers for restaurants and hotels etc come to the market to buy their supplies from 5 a.m. in order to arrange their goods for the day's business.

Q1 Give three types of retail shop that might get supplies from a produce market daily.

Q2 Name the well-known wholesale markets in London, or your local city.

Covent Garden

There are fruit and vegetable wholesale markets in all large towns; London has several, some dating back to medieval times. The best known is Covent Garden. Its original location in central London had to be changed owing to traffic congestion, and "the Garden" is now on a specially designed site beside the Thames.

Fruit, vegetables and flowers are delivered throughout the night by lorry. Some of these supplies come from the countryside, mainly in southern England, but over half are imported from abroad. Covent Garden is one of the largest such markets in the world, with the largest variety of produce.

The wholesalers and porters in the market often come from

Smithfield market

families who have worked there for generations. Rent is paid for stalls which are arranged in sections, e.g. flowers. The market is run by the (nationalised) Covent Garden Market Authority . Prices are very competitive for the retail buyers, who arrive after 5 a.m. to make their day's purchases before 9 a.m. The wholesalers sometimes buy the produce outright from farmers for resale: but often act as agents selling on commission, e.g. for overseas producers.

Q3 Most of the business at Covent Garden is done in nine hours. Describe the main movement of vehicles from midnight to 9 a.m., to and from the market.

Q4 Many imported vegetables arrive by ship every evening for transfer to Covent Garden. Give two examples of where these might come from.

Q5 Fruit is imported from all over the world. Give two examples. Why do some fruits arrive mainly in our winter?

Q6 How do produce wholesalers trade and earn their profit at Covent Garden?

Smithfield

This is the largest dead meat market in the world, with the widest selection. It supplies London, the South East and the Midlands. Half of the sales is of home-killed meat; and the other half is imported from New Zealand, Argentina, Eire, Australia, etc. Meat is brought to Smithfield from the docks or cold stores by lorry, and is unloaded by the Smithfield market porters known as "bummarees". The market operates from 5 a.m. to 1 p.m.

Wholesalers pay rent for their stalls to the Corporation of London who own the market; and also tolls on the weight of meat sold. Buyers are butchers' shops, restaurants, hotels and hospitals; and prices are so competitive that they may vary from hour to hour. Buyers may go themselves to market early; or may telephone orders to a wholesaler with whom they have a special arrangement.

Q7 Give two types of meat and the countries which export them to Britain.

Q8 Who controls Smithfield market and what charges are made to users?

Billingsgate

This is the largest fish market in the world, with the greatest variety. Fish arrives in London by rail from all round our coasts, and is also imported by sea and air. Trading in the market is from 6 a.m. to 3 p.m. but mainly before 9 a.m.

Wholesalers pay rent to the Corporation of London and tolls on the amounts sold. Samples only are displayed on stands and bulk orders are transferred by porters from suppliers' vehicles to buyers' vehicles.

Q9 Imagine you run a fish and chip shop. Describe your morning visit to Billingsgate.

Billingsgate porter wearing the special flat top hat to carry fish boxes.

Vocabulary

Bulk discount
A price reduction for large orders.

Cash and carry wholesalers
Warehouses selling goods to traders at low prices without such services as delivery and credit.

Cash discount
A percentage reduction given for payment within one month of the invoice date.

Commission
Payment to an agent of a percentage of the value of sales made.

Despatch Department
A department arranging packaging and transport of goods for delivery.

Direct selling
Postal sales advertised directly to consumers by wholesalers or manufacturers

Imported
Bought from abroad.

Independent retailers
Smaller retailers not under the control of a large group.

Perishables
Foodstuffs (meat, fish, vegetables) and flowers.

Produce or wholesale markets
Suppliers of perishable foodstuffs to the trade.

Trade or quantity discount
Price reduction depending on the quantity bought by traders.

Voluntary chain
Wholesalers and independent retailers linked together to gain the advantage of large organisations and bulk buying.

Voluntary group
A collection of independent retailers pooling their orders to gain the advantage of bulk discounts.

Wholesaling
To sell in large quantities, e.g. to shops.

4 Banking

Many employers prefer to transfer salaries directly into bank accounts for their employees rather than risk handling large amounts of cash. Many people find it safer and much more convenient to carry a cheque book rather than large sums of cash. Cheques can be easily sent through the post. An account holder can enjoy the wide variety of services provided by banks which enable money to be withdrawn and deposited at any branch of any bank.

Banks may be thought of as markets for money. Money deposited with them by customers is loaned out to others at interest. This provides a valuable service, particularly to businesses.

Sections
 1. Opening a bank account
 2. Safety   Paying into a bank account
 3. Bank giro credit
 4. Paying out of a bank account
    Cash dispensers   Magnetic sorting
 5. Crossings on cheques   Lost cheques   Cheque cards
 6. Clearing a cheque   Bouncing a cheque
 7. Standing orders   Direct debits
 8. Bank statements   Budget accounts
 9. Loans and overdrafts
10. Bank services   Functions of a bank

Section 1

Opening a bank account

"Good morning, Miss Green. Sit down won't you? Now, let's see. You want to open a bank account for the first time?"

"Yes. I've started work at Freemantles, and they pay salaries by cheque."

"Fine. There's some information I'll want from you, and then I'll be able to advise you as to the type of account to suit you. First, we'll complete this form. What is your full name and your address?"

"Jennifer Mary Green, 22 Kirby Street."

"Thank you. Now please fill in your employer's name, and your occupation. And we'll want the names of two "referees", people who can vouch for you. We'll need a specimen of your usual signature, here. You must sign all cheques and letters to the bank in the same way.

"Now perhaps you would let me know whether you intend to do any saving, or do you expect to spend most of your month's salary? We will open a **current** account for you, and let you have a cheque book for withdrawing money and paying bills. But no interest is paid on a current account, as it costs the bank money to service it. For savings, I would suggest a **deposit** account, on which interest is paid."

"Yes, I do want to save a regular amount, towards my holidays, although of course I shall have to take money out of the bank for my living expenses and clothes."

"Right. Then we'll give you a deposit account for your savings as well as a current account. With the deposit account we give you a Pass Book, in which all your deposits and withdrawls are entered. You do not pay cheques from this account—but, of course, you can withdraw your savings when you wish.

"Your cheque book will be sent to you in a couple of days, with your account number and name printed on each cheque. The cheques are crossed as these are safer. Crossed cheques may only be paid into an account. We will show you how to complete one when you want to draw out cash for yourself."

"Thank you."

"Now how much are you going to pay in to open the account?"

"Well, I've got my first pay cheque here, so I'd like to pay that in."

"Fine. I'll fill in this credit slip for you, and we will send you a book of credit slips for paying into your account. When you are writing cheques or credit slips, fill in the counterfoil, so that you have a record of how much is in your account.

"Now, before you go, I must just give you a word of warning, if you have not had a bank account before. Writing cheques may seem very easy, but you have to be careful not to overspend your account, and also not to leave your cheque book lying about!"

"Yes, I'll be very careful."

"Goodbye then, Miss Green, and good luck in your new job."

Q1 Give three reasons why Jennifer is opening a bank account.

Q2 What does the bank manager request from Jennifer as a new account holder?

Q3 What is a current account for, and what is given with it?

Q4 What is a deposit account for, and what is given with it?

Q5 Why should you be careful to fill out the counterfoils in your cheque book?

Q6 Write a paragraph on two dangers of owning a cheque book.

Section 2

Safety

The first reason for putting money into a bank is to keep it safe. The bank has "safes" and "strongrooms". A bank will also keep valuable documents for a client e.g. a will, legal documents, share certificates.

For objects, a **safe deposit box** may be rented. It is kept in the strongroom and only the customer renting the box is allowed the key.

The **night safe** in a bank's outer wall is opened by a key given only to businesses who regularly want to deposit large takings after the bank has closed. The money is locked in a strong leather bag with a note of the amount. This is dropped through the night safe opening and falls down a chute. Next day the bag is opened and the money counted in the presence of a representative of the business and a bank clerk.

Q1 Give two examples of businesses you think might ask for a night safe key and bag.

Q2 Why do you think night safe bags are only opened in the presence of people from both the bank and the business?

Paying into a bank account

A bank needs a written record of anything to do with customers' money, to keep accounts, and in case of any arguments.

Paying in, for the **credit** of an account, is recorded on credit slips. These are printed by a bank to show the date (1); the branch (2); the account to be credited (3 and 4); the amount paid in (6, 7 and 8); and 'paid in by', a record of the name of the person taking the money to the bank (5). Jennifer might be asked to bank the takings of the company she works for. In that case, the money is paid in by her, but the slip is made out to the credit of the company's account.

SPECIMEN CURRENT ACCOUNT CREDIT SLIP

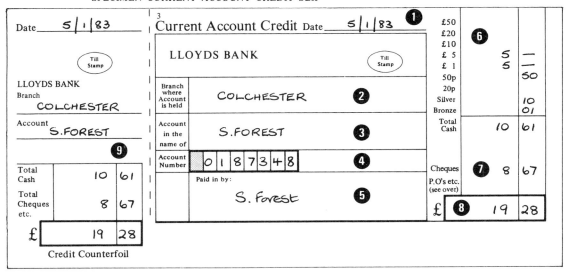

The bank clerk, when she receives the money, will date stamp the credit slip, and also the duplicate or counterfoil kept by the account holder for a record (9).

For the convenience of checking by the bank clerk, cash paid in is divided according to the type and size of notes and coin, e.g. notes of over £1 (£5, £10 or £20); coins of £1, 50p, other silver, or bronze. Against each item the value paid in is shown, e.g. 50 × 50p pieces paid in is shown as £25.

Q3 Draw two columns for £ and p, and label them as in the credit slip above. Then complete them to pay in the money pictured below.

Q4 What information is written on a credit slip?

Q5 Complete a blank credit slip for the account of Jennifer Green, for 10 × £1 coins; 4 × 50p pieces; 8 × 10p pieces; and 10 × 2p pieces. Add the total cash paid in, and carry the total down to the foot of the column. Jennifer paid in the sum herself, on 21 September of this year. Her account number is 6943182, held at the High Street branch, Nottingham.

Q6 Jennifer went to the bank on 22 September to pay in the takings of her employer, Freemantles Ltd. Complete a credit slip to include 10 × £10 notes; 300 × £1 coins; 20 × 50p pieces; 60 × 10p pieces; 30 × 5p pieces; 50 × 2p pieces; 37 × 1p pieces. Total the cash, and add a cheque for £10. Freemantles also use the High Street branch, Nottingham (A/c 2765439).

£5

£1

50p

20p

10p

5p

2p   **1p**

59

Section 3

Bank giro credit

Payment into an account can be made through another branch or bank, as long as details are known of the account holder's "home" bank and the branch that holds his/her signature.

You make out a cheque to your own bank to cover the transfer.

The bank can then take the amount immediately out of your account, to transfer to the bank and branch of the payee.

Alternatively, cash may be paid across the counter of any bank, with a Bank Giro credit form. Then they will transfer payment to the account named. A fee may be charged for the service to non-customers.

If you are a mail order agent, you may be supplied with a book of giro credit forms already printed with the name, bank and branch of the company. You can then pay in your takings at any bank, for transfer to the company's account.

Electricity and Gas Boards, and some other organisations, print a Bank Giro credit form attached to their bills, with the name of their bank and branch already printed on, to make the payment of bills quicker and easier.

If several payments are to be made at the same time, a single cheque can be written to the bank, covering the total of the Bank Giro credit forms. Many employers pay all salaries by Bank Giro credit transfers directly into employees' accounts to save handling and sorting large amounts of cash on pay day. They make a list showing each employee's name, bank and branch and write one cheque to the bank to cover the total monthly salaries. Payments by credit transfer are quicker and safer than paying either in cash or by cheque, which the payee then has to take to a bank to pay in.

Q1 Complete a Bank Giro credit form. On today's date transfer to Lloyds Bank, Forest Hill Branch, for the account of John Player (A/c 7836555), the sum of £10 in one pound coins over the counter of your local bank.

Q2 You forward to your bank by post two Bank Giro credit forms to make payments owing a) of £32.87 to Bradley and Co, who bank at Barclays Bank, Peckham Branch (A/c 5482373) b) of £6.10 to C J Jones, who banks at Midland Bank, Green Lane, Hampstead Branch (A/c 9894432). Make out the necessary forms and covering cheque.

Q3 List three advantages of Bank Giro credit transfers and give three examples of their use.

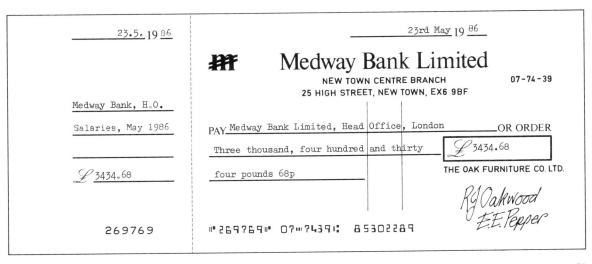

BANK GIRO CREDIT

From MEDWAY BANK LIMITED
25 High Street, New Town, EX6 9BF

DATE 23.5.86

CODE No.	85302289	
TO: BANK BRANCH	Medway Bank Limited Head Office, London	
ACCOUNT AND NUMBER	Barclays Bank, Town Centre, Harlow	
	Baker, Mrs C.V. 12348765	£ 487.59
	Edwards, Mrs G. 55664457	£ 354.77
	Midlands Bank, High, Road, Ilford	
	Dennison, Miss V. 33365347	£ 245.98
	National Westminster Bank, Town Centre, Harlow	
	Baxter, E.J. 89109886	£ 989.67
	Beckett, Miss L. 74032765	£ 589.67
	Cooper, L.M. 88876996	£ 767.00

By order of **THE OAK FURNITURE CO. LTD.** **£** £3434.68

R J Oakwood

23.5. 19 86

Medway Bank, H.O.

Salaries, May 1986

£ 3434.68

269769

23rd May 19 86

Medway Bank Limited
NEW TOWN CENTRE BRANCH 07-74-39
25 HIGH STREET, NEW TOWN, EX6 9BF

PAY Medway Bank Limited, Head Office, London _____ OR ORDER

Three thousand, four hundred and thirty £ 3434.68

four pounds 68p

THE OAK FURNITURE CO. LTD.

R J Oakwood
E.E. Pepper

⑈269769⑈ 07⑈7439⑈ 85302289

Section 4

Paying out of a bank account

Crossed cheques

Bank customers are offered free books of cheques. A bank will only pay money out of an account on receiving an order signed by the account holder. A cheque is a standard order form to the bank, signed by the account holder who is called the **drawer** of the cheque. Two lines drawn across a cheque means that the bank will only pay the money into an account. This may be another bank account, or a savings account.

Each cheque is numbered and tears off from a matching counterfoil or stub. On this you should make a careful note of the amount of each cheque you complete; the name of the payee; and the balance left in your account.

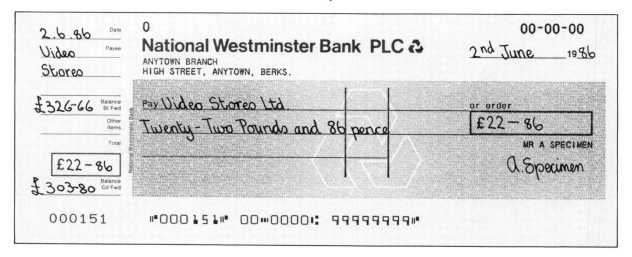

Q1 What information is written on a cheque?

Q2 Complete a blank cheque dated today, ordering your bank to pay £10 to Thomas Grenfell Ltd from your account.

Drawing cash

To cash a cheque you must go to the branch that holds your specimen signature. Only your "home" branch (printed on the top of your cheque book) can compare the signature on the cheque with the specimen held. The crossing on a cheque can be cancelled only by the drawer. "Please pay cash" is written between the lines of the crossing, and signed. The back of the cheque is also signed as a receipt for cash.

Q3 Complete a blank cheque, using today's date, for £25 for your school (towards your school journey).

Q4 You want to draw some money from your account for a day's shopping. Make out a cheque to "Self" dated today, for £40, and open the crossing.

Q5 Where must you go to cash a cheque, and why?

Q6 List the information to be recorded on the counterfoil.

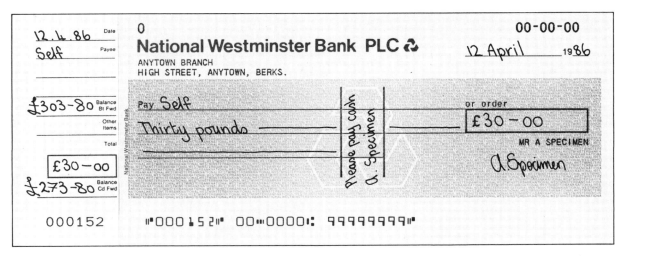

Cash dispensers

Cash dispensers or Service Points are machines which allow customers to draw out money quickly. If the machine is placed on the outside of the bank, it is very useful when the bank is closed. Each customer has a special plastic card to insert, and a secret number which they must key into the machine together with the amount required. If all is in order, a drawer is released containing notes. Deposits and requests for statements of account are also accepted.

Magnetic sorting

At the bottom of a cheque certain numbers are printed in magnetic ink, in a form that can be "read" by a computer. This allows cheques to be sorted automatically at high speed. First, on the left, comes the individual number of the cheque: this is repeated on the counterfoil. Then comes the code number of the bank and the customer's branch. The customer's account number follows. These are what you see on a blank cheque. When the cheque has been made out and someone has paid it into a bank, the amount of the cheque is added in magnetic printing.

Section 5

Crossings on cheques

A crossed cheque must be paid into an account. This may be a bank account, a National Savings Bank (Post Office) account or a building society account etc. It does not have to be paid into the account of the person named on the cheque. The cheque orders the bank to "Pay . . . or Order" i.e. to pay the person named or as they may order. If someone wishes to pass on to someone else a cheque they have been given, the back of the cheque should be signed by the payee named as proof that they have agreed. This is called an **endorsement**. The cheque can then be paid into someone else's account.

Other Crossings are words written on a crossed cheque as a warning to the bank.

The Electricity Board receives hundreds of cheques a day in payment of bills. It will pay these straight into its bank account and will never pass them on to someone else. It therefore asks customers to endorse their cheques "Account payee only" or "A/C payee only". This warns the bank that special enquiries should be made if someone tries to pay the cheque into another account.

You give a cheque to your younger sister, to buy a pair of shoes. You sign and date the cheque: but the details of the name of the shop and the exact amount can only be put in when she has chosen her shoes. You add words, e.g. "Not more than £20" to limit the amount, in case she drops the cheque and someone else picks it up and dishonestly fills it in.

Q1 You have won a prize in a magazine competition, and are sent a crossed cheque for £30. You have not got an account. Can you pass the cheque on to someone else with a bank acocunt in exchange for cash? If so, what should you do?

Q2 Write out a cheque, dated today, to your local gas board for £56.15, and cross it "A/C Payee only".

Q3 You want to give your mother a hairdryer costing £12.00 for her birthday. You are ill so you leave it to your friend to choose when she is shopping. You give her a signed and dated cheque to pay for the hairdryer. What safety precautions might you take?

Lost cheques

If you lose a cheque or a cheque book you should immediately notify the bank, giving the serial number(s). This gives them the chance of stopping payment if anyone tries to use it improperly.

Q4 If you lost a cheque where could you find the serial number?

Cheque cards

Some shops are unwilling to accept a cheque from a customer unknown to them, since the bank will only pay out on a cheque if there is enough money in the account to cover it. **Cheque cards** are issued by some banks to customers who keep a regular amount in their accounts, and this cheque card guarantees any cheque up to £50. Most shops will accept a cheque under £50 from a customer with a cheque card. Also with this card any branch of any bank will cash a cheque for the holder up to £50.

Q5 Why are shops sometimes reluctant to accept cheques in payment for goods?

Q6 What are the benefits of holding a cheque card?

Section 6

Clearing a cheque

Mrs West, whose account is at Lloyds Bank, gives a cheque to Mr East who pays it into his account at Barclays Bank. Barclays are now holding a Lloyds cheque; and the amount must be added to Mr East's account at Barclays and taken out of Mrs West's account at Lloyds.

1. Each Barclays branch every day passes all cheques paid in for accounts in other banks and branches, up to Barclays' headquarters for sorting.
2. Here, cheques from other Barclays branches are separated from those from other banks, which are passed on to the Bankers' Clearing House in batches, with a summary of the amount owing from each bank.
3. At the Clearing House all batches of cheques passing between the banks are sorted and listed, to find out the total that one bank owes another at the end of each day's dealings. These daily totals are passed to the Bank of England, the Bankers' bank, for adjustment between the accounts of each bank, held there.
4. The Clearing House pass on the sorted cheques to the headquarters of the banks printed on them. They in turn sort them and send them to the correct "home" branch.
5. When the cheque reaches its home branch the money can be deducted from the account of Mrs West, after her signature and balance have been checked. The branch sends customers regular statements of payments into and out of their accounts. The process of clearing a cheque takes 3–4 working days.

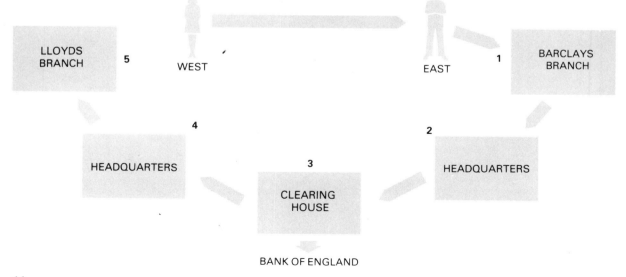

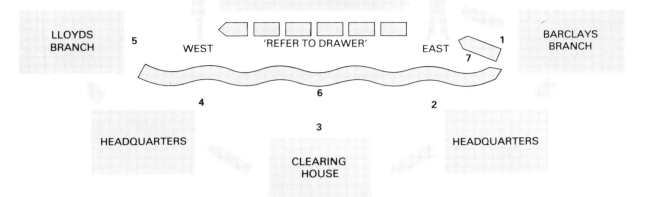

Bouncing a Cheque

If there is not enough money in an account to cover a cheque, or if it has not been correctly made out, the bank may refuse to pay it. The cheque is "bounced" straight back to the branch where it was paid in, as payment into their customer's account has not been completed.

The bank that receives back a "bounced" cheque marks it "**Refer to Drawer**" (*R.D.*) and returns it to the customer who paid it in. It is then up to the customer to refer back to the drawer, i.e. the person who signed it, to make new arrangements for the paying of the debt.

Q1 Why does a branch receive cheques of other banks every day?

Q2 Why are cheques sent to the Clearing House?

Q3 Who is the Bankers' bank?

Q4 Copy the clearing diagram. Number and list the stages of clearing a cheque.

Q5 What action is taken when a cheque reaches its "home" branch?

Q6 What is meant by a "bounced" cheque? Describe in your own words what happens to a "bounced" cheque?

All banks sort cheques by computer; and all customers' bank accounts are held on and updated by computer. Statements are also completed by computer. Here, information is being viewed on Visual Display Units which are connected directly to the bank's computer.

Section 7

Standing orders

Sometimes you want to make the payment of a fixed sum at regular intervals, e.g. a hire purchase instalment, or your rent or rates. To save having to remember to make out a cheque on the right date, a Standing Order may be given to your bank. This instructs them to transfer from your account a stated amount at regular intervals to the bank and branch of the payee, the beneficiary.

After a transfer is made into a company's account, they are then notified by their bank in their next statement and they will tick off the payment in their records.

BiS   **STANDING ORDER MANDATE**

To _Midland Bank Limited_ ... **1**

Address _Town Centre Harlow_ ...

	Bank	Branch Title (not address)	Code Number	
Please Pay	Barclays	Bishops Stortford	20-09-59	**2**
		Beneficiary	Account Number	
for the credit of	Ray's Hi-fi, High Street, Bishops Stortford		3 0 7 4 8 8 2 1	**3**
	Amount in figures	Amount in words		
†the sum of	£10	Ten pounds		**4**

	Date and amount of 1st payment			Date and frequency	
commencing	1-7-86 *now	£10	and thereafter every	month	**5**
	Date and amount of last payment				
*until	1-1-88	£10			**6**
quoting the reference	—		and debit my/~~our~~ account accordingly		

*This instruction cancels any previous order in favour of the beneficiary named above, under this reference
†If the amount of the periodic payments vary they should be incorporated in a schedule overleaf

Special instructions _____

Signature(s) _R.V. Jones_   Date _20·6·86_

Title and number of account to be debited   _R.V. JONES_ | 8 0 6 5 5 5 3 2 |

*Delete if not applicable

Note: The Bank will not undertake to
    (i)   make any reference to Value Added Tax or pay a stated sum "plus VAT"
    (ii) advise payer's address to beneficiary
    (iii) advise beneficiary of inability to pay
    (iv) request beneficiary's banker to advise beneficiary of receipt.

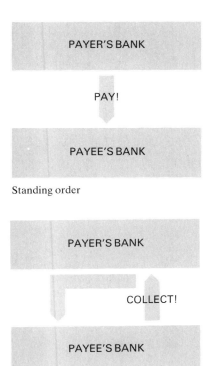

Standing order

Direct debit

The Bank Giro sign
symbolising the transfer of
payments between banks

Direct debits

Some companies (e.g. insurance companies) may have lists of a large number of payments due on a particular date. They find it easier and quicker for their clerks to be able to tick off this whole list when they are ready. They therefore ask a customer to complete a Direct Debit form. This is an order by the customer to the bank to transfer payment from his account when requested by the company.

Q1 The Standing Order illustration covers instalments due on an HP (hire purchase) agreement. What is the amount of the instalment? For what period is it to be paid? What is the total sum that will have been transferred after the last payment?

Q2 Complete a Standing Order (1) for your bank (Midland, Town Centre, Harlow), for your rent of £30 (4) a month (5) to Harlow Town Council (3) who bank at National Westminster Bank (2) (Prince Road, Harlow), account number 07615389. The payment should be transferred on the first of every month, starting 1 January next year. Instead of a final date write "Until further notice". Sign the form.

Q3 Why would a Standing Order be suitable for your monthly trade union subscription but not for your quarterly electricity bill?

Q4 Which three forms instruct a bank to transfer payment direct from your account to another bank account?

BiS   **DIRECT DEBITING MANDATE**

The Manager

Midland   Bank
Town Centre
Harlow

I/We authorise you until further notice in writing to charge to my/our account with you on or immediately after **1ˢᵗ March 1986** (date) **monthly** (frequency) unspecified amounts which **Sunshine Life Assurance PLC** (originator) may debit thereto by Direct Debit.

This Mandate cancels all previous Standing Order/Direct Debiting Mandates in favour of

_____ (originator) under the following Reference No. _____

Date of first payment on or within one calendar month from **1ˢᵗ March 1986**

Signature **R. B. Jones**

Name of account
to be debited

R. B. JONES

| 0 | 0 | 1 | 4 | 5 | 6 | 7 | 8 |

Reference No. **JON/548/86**

Date **12 December 1985**

Instructions cannot be accepted to charge direct debits to a Deposit or Savings Account.

Section 8

Bank statements

BiS

IN ACCOUNT WITH

TITLE OF ACCOUNT Mrs. C. J. Jones

BANK OF EDUCATION

BRANCH HOMETOWN

ACCOUNT NUMBER 89253750

STATEMENT NUMBER 12

DATE	PARTICULARS		PAYMENTS	RECEIPTS	BALANCE
	Balance Forward				
1 DEC					167.03
2 DEC		626	20.00		147.03
4 DEC		BG	47.50		99.53
9 DEC		627	20.00		79.53
10 DEC		629	16.75		62.78
12 DEC		SO	9.15		53.63
16 DEC		630	20.00		33.63
18 DEC		SO	4.20		29.43
19 DEC		628	4.50		24.93
20 DEC		CH	2.00		22.93
23 DEC		631	20.00		2.93
29 DEC		632	8.30		5.37 DR
30 DEC		BG		300.00	294.63

ABBREVIATIONS

BGC Bank Giro Credit
DD Direct Debit
CD Cash Dispenser

DIV Dividend
CHS Charges
ADV Separately Advised

O/D or DR Overdrawn Balance
SO Standing Order
TFR Inter-Account Transfer

Q1 Look at the bank statement above. How often do you think it is sent to the account holder?

Q2 Mrs Jones' salary is transferred directly into her account every month by credit transfer from her employer.
a) What is the date?
b) What is the amount of this transfer?
c) What was her bank balance at the end of the previous month?
d) What was her bank balance after her salary payment?

Q3 The numbers opposite payments show the serial numbers of cheques. Mrs Jones writes her cheques in sequence, in her cheque book: but they do not appear in the same order on her statement. Why do you think this is?

Q4 Bank charges may be deducted from an account twice a year (e.g. June and December) if the account has been overdrawn. Charges depend on the average balance in an account and the amount of servicing or bank work down for a customer. How much in bank charges has been deducted from Mrs Jones' account?

Q5 Traditionally any bank balance in debit instead of in credit, i.e. overdrawn, was printed in red. If you owed money it was called "being in the red". Bank statements are now printed by computer, in black throughout. Mrs Jones overdrew her account at the end of the month. Say
 a) by how much
 b) how this is shown.

Q6 Why do you think the bank allowed Mrs Jones to overdraw her account without "bouncing" her last cheque?

Q7 Make up a story to explain all the payments into and out of Mrs Jones' account in the month. (Pay particular attention to the items paid by credit transfer or standing order.)

Budget Accounts

A **Budget Account** can be arranged with a bank to even out the difficulty of heavy demands for payment falling in certain months, e.g. with quarterly bills, or an annual season ticket. Instead, the customer makes a regular monthly payment to the bank by standing order. On a Budget Account form the customer puts down an estimate of her year's regular bills. The total is then divided by 12 to give an even monthly spread. When the bills listed arrive, the customer pays them by special budget account cheques provided by the bank, which are cleared at whatever time of the year they arrive, whatever the customer's bank balance at the time. At the end of the year it can be seen whether the customer over or under-estimated the total, and payment between the bank and the customer is adjusted. A charge is made for this arrangement.

Q8 Why are a householder's bills much heavier in certain months?

Q9 What is the point of a Budget Account with a bank?

Q10 How does a bank know, when cheques are being cleared for payment, which refer to expenses it has agreed to "spread out" or budget for a customer?

Account   Customer's Copy

ule of Estimated Annual Commitments

Payment	Estimated Maximum Annual Expenditure £ p		Month(s) when payment(s) become due
Rates	500	00	APRIL + NOV.
Rate			
ine	420	00	FEB. MAY AUG. NOV.
ty			
cluding Oil and Coal)			
Fees			
urance	110	00	MAY
and Contents Insurance	90	00	JUNE
urance			
ence			
ng and Maintenance Agreements	24	00	OCTOBER
Ticket			
on Licence	58	00	SEPTEMBER
s			
Subscriptions	22	00	JANUARY
g			
as Expenses	50	00	DECEMBER
stimated Annual ture	1,274	00	
credit balance forward	—		
al (minimum £500)	1,274	00	
rvice Charge of £35 to ver first £500 thereafter per £50 of expenditure any part thereof	51	00	
vings	49	00	
	1,374	00	
hereby authorised, of transfer from Current t, being 1/12th of the	114	50	

NB
If the schedule is exceeded a further service charge will become payable — see condition 4

s available on the reverse of this oting payment details.)

Account Number 1 0 2 5 3 0 7 7

Account Number 1 0 2 5 3 0 4 2

1.11.85 Signature(s) J. Brown

Section 9

Loans and overdrafts

Money left with a bank does not lie idle in the vaults. Other people and businesses are prepared to pay interest to borrow sums from the bank for a short period. This is how banks make their profit. Sums are borrowed in two ways: a) loans; b) overdrafts.

Loans are arranged for a certain sum, for a certain period, at a fixed rate of interest. For example £2,000 loaned for two years at 15 per cent per annum (a year), to buy a new vehicle. The sum, plus interest, is repaid by instalments during the period.

Overdrafts are arranged as a limit, say £500, up to which accounts may be overdrawn. Interest is only charged on any amount actually overdrawn in any month. It is included in bank charges.

Many people and businesses have overdrafts at some time. For example, a manufacturer of fireworks may have difficulty in finding enough money for wages and supplies during the summer and may seek a bank overdraft to tide the business over until the main sales in November. A retailer may want a loan to convert a shop to self-service. A customer may need help to buy a new car; or a "bridging loan" between buying a new house and selling the old one.

Bank managers become very experienced in advising on how much debt repayment (e.g. as a percentage of income) an individual

or business can manage without running into difficulties. They will want to know what other debts are already being carried by someone seeking an overdraft or loan. They will discuss what the money is for; how much is needed, and for how long; and how repayment (with interest) is to be made. They must be satisfied that the money will be used to advantage; and the debt to the bank can be repaid from future income or from the likely future profits of a business. Bank managers are conscious that they are using depositors' money for which they are responsible.

A bank loan will be repaid probably by monthly instalments. An overdraft may be cleared by payment into the bank account of the next month's salary, or profits.

Various lending schemes may be offered, such as a credit limit as a multiple of a regular monthly payment to the bank, e.g. monthly payment of £4 allows × 20 credit = £80.

Banks traditionally "lend short", i.e. they like to have money repaid within a short period, say two years, and on a regular basis, by instalments. However, banks now consider longer loans to businesses; and will provide long-term loans for property e.g. 20 years, on a mortgage.

Q1 If you have a bank loan of £3,000 for one year at 12 per cent per annum interest, how much would you have to repay in total? How much would this be monthly?

Q2 Where does a bank get the money to lend people?

Q3 Name two forms of bank lending: explain each in your own words.

Q4 Taking the examples above as a guide, give two other circumstances in which an individual or a business might seek a bank loan or overdraft.

Q5 What four questions might be asked by a bank manager of someone wanting a loan or overdraft? What is the aim of the questioning?

Security may be asked for by a bank to cover the value of a loan or overdraft. A security is something of value that can be held by the bank, and could be sold as a last resort to repay the loan. Suitable as security are savings certificates; premium bonds; stocks and share certificates; life assurance policies; or the deeds of a house. Alternatively the bank may ask you for a guarantee from a friend or relative, who would be responsible for repayment if you defaulted.

Q6 Explain in your own words what is meant by a security.

Q7 Give three examples of what might be considered security for a bank loan of £3,000.

Credit cards

Credit is a form of loan. Banks are associated with credit card schemes, although these are run by separate companies in which each bank has a stake, e.g. Barclays in Barclaycard; Lloyds, National Westminster, Midland and others in Access (see p. 170). You do not have to be a customer of one bank to hold a particular credit card. Banks' shareholding in credit card companies means they control a system of arranging non-cash payments and credit which is convenient for the customer. It parallels a cheque-and-overdraft system, while not overburdening the banks; and allows for separate, and international development.

Q8 Give two examples of the close association between banks and credit card companies.

Section 10

Bank services

People turn to their Bank Manager for discussion and **advice** on all kinds of financial matters, e.g. loans, investments, insurance, taxation, business risks.

A bank is often given as a reference, e.g. on hire purchase contracts.

Banks have large Executor and Trustee Departments.

Executors of wills see to all the legal and money business after a death.

Trustees manage money affairs entrusted to them on behalf of somebody else, e.g. an orphan.

Travellers' cheques and foreign currencies are provided by a bank for travellers going abroad. The customer pays the bank in advance for travellers' cheques guaranteed for payment by the bank. These are then acceptable all over the world.

Exporters are provided with many services by banks, such as business introductions to foreign banks, arrangements for collection of payment overseas, and/or transfers to this country of payments made abroad. Loans are made on special terms to help exporters. Information and statistics useful in foreign trade are published.

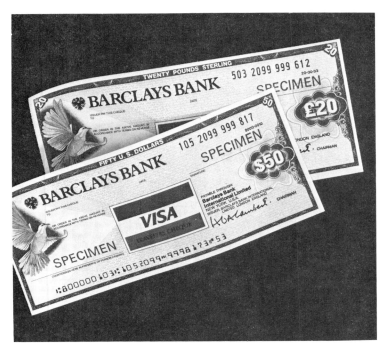

Q1 Give three types of advice you might seek from your bank manager as
    a) a private individual
    b) an owner of a business.

Q2 A man with a young family is making his will to arrange his money affairs for when he dies. What bank services might he call on and for what purpose?

Q3 You are going on a school journey to France for two weeks. How might the bank help you over the question of spending money?

Q4 Give three ways in which banks give special help to exporters.

Functions of a bank

```
                        BANKS
        ┌───────────┬─────────────┬───────────┐

    Safety      Transfer       Loans        Other
                  of                       services
                payments
```

Q5 Draw the above diagram and add two examples under each heading.

Q6 Using the diagram as a guide, make a list of what the bank does for the individual customer.

Q7 Which items in your list would not apply to businesses; but what services would be added?

Vocabulary

Bank balance
The amount in a bank account.

Bank Giro credit
A method of quickly transferring payments directly from the account of the payer to that of the payee.

Bank statement
A document sent regularly by a bank to each customer, listing payments into or out of the account for the period, with a running balance after each entry.

"Bounced" cheque
A cheque on which the bank has refused to make payment, e.g. because there is not enough money in the account to cover it.

Cash dispensers
Machines for withdrawing money, often on the outside of banks. Deposits and requests for statement of account may also be made.

Cheque cards
Bank cards showing a customer's signature and guaranteeing cheques up to £50.

Clearing
The banking process of transferring payments between accounts i.e. to the payee from the payer.

Credit balance
An account into which more money has been paid than withdrawn.

Crossed cheques
Cheques crossed by a double line, which must be paid into an account.

Current account
An account with a Bank for paying money in and out quickly and easily.

Debit balance
An account from which more money has been withdrawn than has been paid in (overdrawn).

Deposit account
A savings account paying interest on money left undisturbed for a period.

Direct debit
Agreement to allow the payees to collect payment to themselves from the payer's account when requested.

Drawer
The account holder who writes or draws up a cheque.

Endorsement
The signature, on the back of a cheque, of the named payee.

Executors
Persons named in someone's will as responsible for seeing that their wishes are carried out.

Loan
Money lent for a certain period at a fixed rate of interest.

Overdrafts
Permission to withdraw money up to an agreed limit beyond money paid in to the account.

Payee
The name of the person for whom payment is intended.

RD
"Refer to drawer" — written on a bounced cheque before it is returned to the customer.

Referees
People who know you well and who can recommend your reliability or answer for your honesty.

Security
Something of value, e.g. house ownership papers or deeds, or life insurance policies that can be held by a bank until a loan is repaid.

Service Points
Machines for withdrawing or depositing money.

Standing order
An order to transfer, to another account, a fixed sum at regular intervals.

Trustees
Persons who manage the money left in trust to someone else e.g. an orphan.

5 Other methods of payment

A number of ways of transferring payment are provided through the Post Office. These range from the familiar postal order to the various services of the National Girobank.

A number of official payments (television licences, or pensions) may also be made or received through Post Offices.

Sections
1. National Girobank   Transcash form
2. National Girobank   Transfer/Deposit forms
   Girocheques
3. National Girobank   Withdrawals   Other services
4. Other payments through the Post Office

Section 1

GIRO 'CIRCLE'

National girobank

The word Giro means a circle. The circular diagram illustrates the National Girobank system. Details of all Giro accounts are kept on an enormous computer at Bootle, Merseyside. Money transferred between one account and another inside the computer is the quickest method there is of payment.

All the public utilities (electricity, gas and water boards) include a Giro transfer form at the foot of their bills, with their Giro account number already printed on it. To pay the bill the customer only has to insert his own Giro account number, and sign and date the form; or pay in cash over the Post Office counter.

The National Girobank is operated through the Post Office. Post Office branches are so numerous, with opening hours longer than those of banks, that this is very convenient for the public.

Every Post Office holds Girobank Business Account directories giving the names and account numbers of all Giro account holders.

Q1 What is the meaning of the word Giro?
Q2 What makes transfers of payment between Giro accounts so fast?
Q3 How do public utilities help their customers to pay through National Girobank?
Q4 If you have a National Girobank account, how would you complete the Transfer Form, to settle your bill?
Q5 If you have not got a National Girobank account, how could you use the Giro form to pay your water rates?
Q6 Name an advantage of a National Girobank account over a bank account.
Q7 How could you find out whether a company to whom you owe money had a Girobank account, so that you could pay over the Post Office counter?

Transcash Form

The Transcash Form is completed at a Post Office branch by anyone without a Girobank account who wishes to pay an account holder. Then cash paid across the counter settles the bill. A fee of 40p is charged (but you save the cost of an envelope and postage; or a bus fare to pay the bill in person). Any bill can be paid in this way, if the company has a Girobank account.

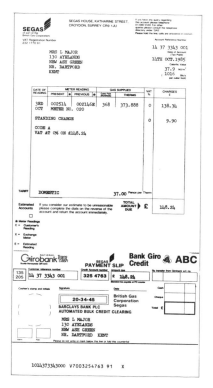

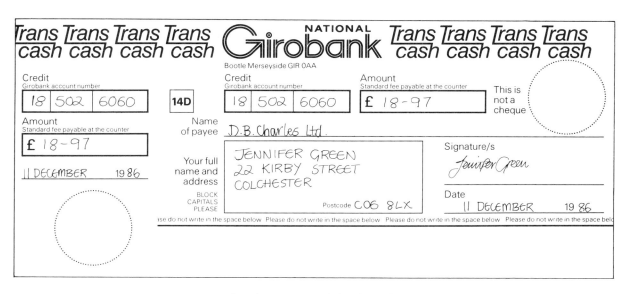

On the reverse of the form is space for a message that may be sent with the payment.

Q8 You owe £32.60 to D.F.D.S. Travel. Look up their Girobank account number from the extract of the Giro directory reproduced below.

Q9 Trace the Transcash Form above and complete it for the payment in Q8.

Q10 What do you think would go in the dotted circle on the right of the form?

Q11 You owe this sum for the deposit on your holiday in Copenhagen, Tour No 562, starting 17 June. What message would you write on the reverse of the Inpayment Form?

D.B.M. Electronics, 113 Strafford Gate
Potters Bar 38 704 4000
D. & C. Electriks, Engs, 32–34 Robert st
Newport-on-Tay 19 091 0003
D.E.R. Ltd,
Area Acctnt
Apex Ho Twickenham rd Feltham 36 800 0001
213 Lord st Southport 613 9620
Do. 618 8621
St. Albans ho 181 The Parade Watford 307 3025
S. England, London W, London S.W, London S.E,
Apex ho Twickenham rd Feltham 306 2414
South, South East, South West, West,
Apex ho Twickenham rd Feltham 319 2415
Scotland, N.E. England, Yorkshire, Fargate ct
Fargate, Sheffield 315 2413
Area Manager Fargate ct Fargate
Sheffield 309 2410
D.F.D.S. Travel, Prop The Danish Tourist Bureau Ltd,
Mariner ho Pepys st London 553 4151
D. & G. Discount Supplies Ltd, Wlppr & Hdwre,
5 New Broadway Hampton rd
Hampton Hl, Hampton 33 703 0006
D-H-J. Cut Linings Ltd, 42–42a Tallon rd

Section 2

National girobank

Transfer/Deposit forms

Anyone over 15 may open a Girobank account with a deposit of at least £1. An application form is filled in, with specimen signatures. The Girobank Centre at Bootle then send the new account holder a pack of "personalised" stationery. Each form is printed with the account holder's new account number and with his name and address. The Transfer/Deposit Form is used for paying money into the account (making a deposit); or transferring payment to another Girobank account. If you wish to pay some more money into your own account, the world "Self" should be written across the box headed "Credit Account Number". The amount is written in words and figures. Printed envelopes with free postage are provided for posting Transfer/Deposit Forms to the Girobank Centre in Bootle.

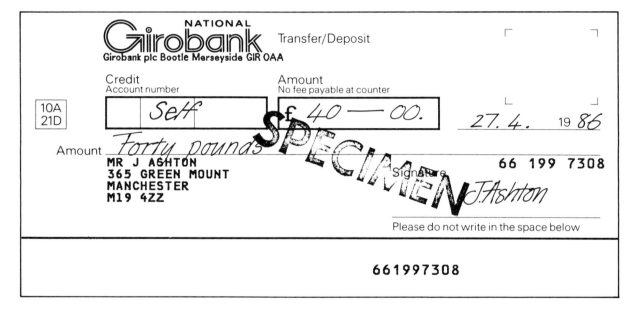

Q1 How old do you have to be to open a Girobank account and what is the minimum deposit?

Q2 What has to be completed to open a Girobank account?

Q3 What is printed of a personal nature on each account holder's stationery?

Q4 List the entries to be made on a Transfer/Deposit Form to pay a further £20 into your account.

Girocheques

All money held in National Girobank Accounts is available for use by the Government. Transfers between one account and another are completed by the computer and do not affect the total funds held "in the circle", in the Girobank.

Girocheques are provided for making payments to people who do not have a Girobank account, i.e. paying outside the circle. Girocheques can be crossed (like other cheques) and sent direct to the payee for payment into an account.

If the person being paid does not have a bank or other account, and wants cash, the Girocheque should be first sent to the Girobank for the account to be debited (i.e. the money deducted). The Girocheque will be sent on from Bootle to the person being paid, who will then be able to cash it at a local post office.

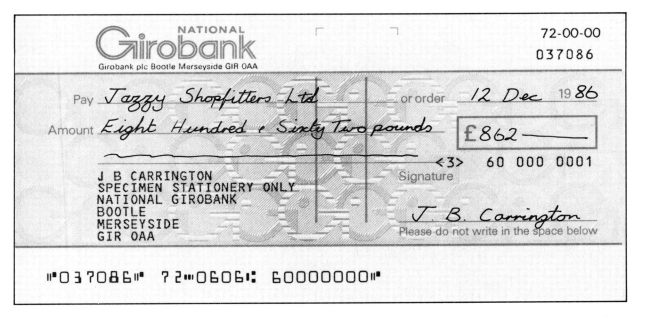

Q5 What use is made of the money held in Girobank accounts?

Q6 How is the total money in the Giro circle affected by
a) a deposit
b) a transfer
c) a Girocheque?

Q7 For what kind of payment would you use a Girocheque?

Q8 What is the effect of crossing a Girocheque?

Q9 If the person being paid does not have a bank or other account,
a) where should the Girocheque be sent?
b) where may payment be received?

Q10 Trace the Girocheque above. Complete it for payment of £15 to Tom Fitzgerald. Use today's date.

Section 3

National girobank

Withdrawals

Money can be withdrawn from a Girobank account by cashing a Girocheque. Each account holder may name two Post Office branches who will hold his specimen signature, and be prepared to cash his Girocheques. Up to £50 may be withdrawn every other day.

Guarantee Card

A plastic guarantee card may be obtained. It shows your signature and enables up to £50 to be withdrawn at any Post Office branch, or £100 at your named branch. It also guarantees payment on Girocheques or transfer forms up to £50 when used for purchases in a shop.

Q1 How may you take money out of your Girobank account for your personal use?

Q2 How much money can be withdrawn at a time and how often?

Q3 What are the advantages of holding a Girobank guarantee card?

Standing Orders

A form can be completed to arrange for Girobank to pay a regular amount at regular intervals out of an account, e.g. for rent, or hire purchase repayments.

International Payments

Other European countries operate Girobank systems through post offices as in Britain. Payments between countries can be made through a National Girobank Transcash form.

Q5 What is a Girobank Standing Order? When might it be used?

Q6 How might payment be made to another country through the National Girobank?

Q7 Draw the National Girobank emblem.

Statement of Account

Every time a deposit is made by an account holder, the Girobank computer automatically prints a Statement of Account for sending out. A statement is also sent after any credit (transfer into an account), or after 10 debits (payments out).

STATEMENT OF ACCOUNT   **NATIONAL**   G70▶

Number   64 653 2170   20 Dec 86   **Girobank**   Serial 009

Bootle Merseyside GIR OAA

VAT registration number 243 1700 02

Summary			Transactions		DEBITS			£
previous balance	30 Nov 86	£106.40	3DEC	S	2143211	WST BDG SOC	25.00
total debits		84.02	5DEC	G	0009	GIROCHEQUE	15.00
total credits		25.00	5DEC	S	6139627	TV RENT CO	3.40
current balance	20 Dec 86	£ 47.38	18DEC	T	6130008	NW ELEC BD	16.50
			18DEC	G	0010	GIROCHEQUE	4.00
			18DEC	G	0011	SELF	20.00
					FEES		0.12
					CREDITS		
MR J ASHTON			20DEC	D	SELF		25.00
6 RAVENBOURNE GARDENS							
LIVERPOOL							
L20 9LG							

C Cheque   T Transfer   S Standing Order
D Deposit   TC Transcash   A Automatic
OD Overdrawn   DD Direct Debit   debit transfer

Enquiries: Please contact your Regional Office, where this has been notified to you, otherwise, National Girobank, Bootle, Merseyside, GIR OAA, (telephone 051-928 8112).

Q8 Look at the statement above
  a) What is Mr. Ashton's account number?
  b) How much was in the account on 30th November 1986?
  c) What Girocheques were paid out between 3rd to 18th December?
  d) What standing order payments were made in December?
  e) For how much was the electricity bill and how was it settled?
  f) How did Mr. Ashton top up his account?
  g) What was his balance on 20th December?

Other Services

National Girobank is steadily increasing the number of services offered to account holders. Foreign currency and traveller's cheques may be bought from Giro through a Post Office and will be posted to the account holder's address. Those with a salary-through-Giro account may apply for personal loans.

Q9 How may Giro help those travelling abroad?
Q10 To what type of customers are Girobank loans available?

Section 4

Other payments through the post office

Postal Orders

Postal orders may be bought at any post office. This is the most convenient way of sending money by post for anyone without a bank or Giro account, as they can be cashed at any post office or paid into an account.

Postal orders can be bought for amounts from 25p to £10.

Poundage (a fee) is charged of 21p for orders from 25p to £1, and 32p for orders from £2 to £10.

Apart from personal use of postal orders for such things as birthday presents, they are also used regularly in business, e.g. for football pools, postal sales. A postal order may be crossed (like a cheque); it must then be paid into an account.

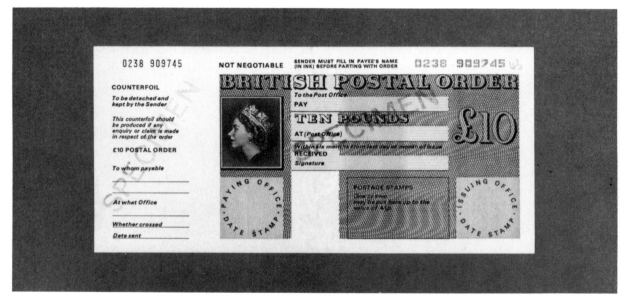

Q1 What are the lowest and highest values of postal orders?

Q2 What is poundage?

Q3 What total would you pay over the counter for the following postal order purchases

    a) one PO for £5;

    b) four POs for £1;

    c) three POs for 50p?

Q4 Give two types of business that receive many postal orders from customers.

Q5 What is the effect of crossing a postal order?

Cash on Delivery

The Post Office provides a service whereby the postman delivering a parcel will collect payment for the goods (COD) of up to £350. The Post Office charges a fee, and transfers the payment collected to the seller.

Licences, Pensions etc.

The post office is used by a number of government departments for making or collecting payments. Payment may be made over a post office counter for a television licence, citizens band radio licence, driving licence renewals and road tax. Payments may be received at a post office for State pensions, maternity benefit, child benefit, sick benefit, supplementary benefit etc.

Q7 What does COD mean?

Q8 How does the COD service work?

Q9 Give three licence payments that may be made over the post office counter.

Q10 Give three payments made by the post office on behalf of government departments.

Vocabulary

COD
"Cash on Delivery" — a service where payment is made to the postman when goods are delivered.

Giro
A circular system used in banking to show the transfer of payments within the system.

Guarantee Card
Issued by Girobank to guarantee withdrawals from any Post Office or payments by Girocheque up to £50.

"Personalised" stationery
Forms printed with the account holder's name and account number.

Poundage
A fee charged by the Post Office on postal orders and telegraphic money orders.

Public utilities
Services used by everyone, e.g. electricity, gas and water.

6 Insurance

Insurance is nowadays a part of everyday life. Young people and students may seek the protection of insurance for things they own — a guitar, a motor cycle or a tape recorder. This provides money as compensation in the event of loss or damage.

A family man will seek insurance protection for his house and car; and may take out life insurance to provide money for his family when he dies.

Certain risks, such as unemployment and sickness, are covered by National Insurance.

Businesses, trading goods round the world, rely on the protection of cargo insurance.

Britain is a world leader in the insurance market, and earns much foreign currency by the sale of insurance policies overseas.

Sections
1. Spreading the risk
2. Getting insured
3. Principles of Insurance
4. What can be insured?
5. Common insurances
6. Household Insurance
7. Business policies
8. Lloyds of London
9. Life insurance
10. Choosing life cover   Insurance funds   Advantages of insurance
11. National Insurance

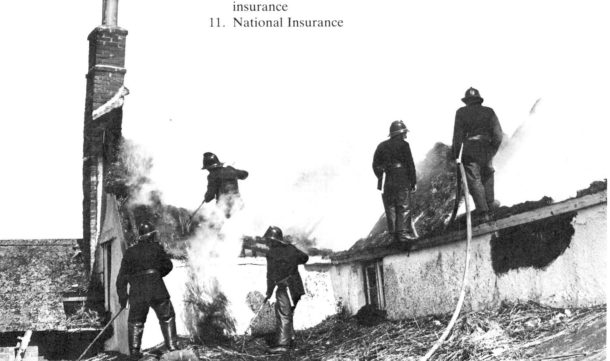

Section 1

Spreading the risk

Insurance protects people against financial loss, by paying compensation. Where does the money come from? Insurance companies collect contributions from many people who want to be "covered", so that the few who suffer loss may be paid. The contributions for this protection, called **premiums**, are paid into a fund or pool.

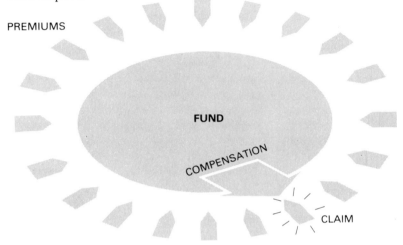

People are glad to pay a small sum regularly rather than run the risk of suffering a really large loss from an accident. This could be disastrous for one person, without the help of others who have contributed to the pool. "Spreading the risk" means sharing the risk of loss in this way.

The insurance business is based on a mountain of statistics. Records are kept of how many disasters and accidents of different types there are in a year, and how much compensation is claimed. An insurance company must know the amount it is likely to have to pay out yearly and make sure that it collects enough in premiums to cover the payments out. Figures on fires have been collected since the Great Fire of London in 1666.

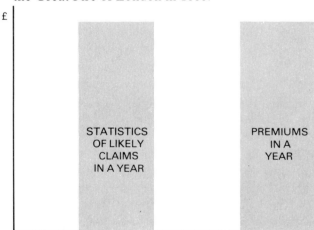

If it is not possible to judge the extent of a risk or the size of claims, because of lack of statistics, an insurance company may refuse to give insurance cover. **Uninsurable risks** include such things as shoplifting, business profits, change of fashion.

A modern industrial society represents wealth in buildings and machinery built up over centuries. Nowadays, a single construction may cost millions of pounds, e.g. an oil rig or a giant liner. Insurance is vital in protecting the enormous amount of investment involved (as it is in protecting a person's possessions).

Q1 Copy the diagram on Spreading the Risk. What is meant by this title?

Q2 Why do you think the cost of motor insurance premiums has risen over the past few years?

Q3 Why are accident statistics so important to the insurance industry?

Q4 How do insurance companies decide how much premium they will charge to cover a particular risk?

Q5 Why do you think the cost of insuring a Jumbo Jet is so high?

Q6 Why is the insurance industry far more important in an industrial society than in an under-developed country?

Section 2

Getting insured

The Four P's of Insurance

Protection is sought against various risks which would cause financial loss.

Proposal form is completed by someone wishing to be insured. The form asks questions which will enable the insurance company to estimate the risk, e.g. "What material is your house built of?"

Premium is the regular payment made weekly, monthly, quarterly or yearly to buy protection.

Policy is the contract between the insurance company and the insured person. The policy comes into force from the payment of the first premium.

Proposal for Motor Cycle Insurance

Div	Dist	Agency

THIS IS AN IMPORTANT DOCUMENT because it is the basis of the Insurance contract between you and PEARL ASSURANCE PUBLIC LIMITED COMPANY besides governing the premium and terms of the Policy.

PLEASE (1) ANSWER ALL QUESTIONS (2) USE BLOCK LETTERS (3) TICK ☑ BOXES AS APPROPRIATE

PARTICULARS OF PROPOSER

Surname Mr/Mrs/Miss _____ First Names _____

Address _____

Local/Regional Admin-District _____ County _____ Post Code _____

Occupation(s) _____ Date of Birth _____
(including any part time occupation)

COVER REQUIRED

Comprehensive	With £30 Accidental Damage Excess ☐
Comprehensive	With £50 Accidental Damage Excess ☐
Comprehensive	With £75 Accidental Damage Excess ☐
Third Party Fire and Theft	☐
Third Party Only	☐

PARTICULARS OF THE MOTOR CYCLE TO BE INSURED

Make	Registration Letters and Number	Cubic Capacity (cc)	Year of Manufacture	Seating Capacity of Sidecar (if any)	Estimate of value Cycle £	Sidecar £

1. Will the motor cycle be used solely for your social, domestic and business purposes? YES ☐ NO ☐ If 'NO' state other uses _____

2. Do you desire the policy to exclude use of any motor cycle unless a side-car is attached? YES ☐ NO ☐ If 'YES' the premium will be reduced and the policyholder will not be insured whilst riding a solo machine.

3. Are you the owner of the motor cycle and is it registered in your name? YES ☐ NO ☐ If 'NO' give full details

PROPOSER'S CLAIMS/DRIVING EXPERIENCE

4. Have you had any accidents or losses in the last 3 years? YES ☐ NO ☐ If 'YES' give number and date(s) [____]

5. (a) Do you hold a current licence to drive a motor cycle of the type proposed? YES ☐ NO ☐ If 'NO' give full details

(b) Have you held a full UK licence to drive a motor cycle of the type proposed for at least 1 year? YES ☐ NO ☐

TO BE COMPLETED BY THE AGENT

(a) Cover — Points Column

Comprehensive		T.P.		
£30	£50	£75	F. & T.	T.P.O.
30	29	27	7	1

(b) Rating District

SI	1 & 2	3	4	5 & 6	7
-5	0	1	2	4	13

(c) Motor Cycle

c.c	0-50	51-100	101-200	201-300	301-400	401-500	501+
Solo	0	9	31	43	53	67	91
Side car	0	9	16	22	27	39	31

(d) Age of Proposer (or Additional Driver if younger)

16-18	19-21	22-24	25-29	30+
36	28	19	10	0

(e) Additional Drivers (maximum of 2 if cc 51+)

cc	None	1	2
0-50	0	0	0
51+	0	6	12

(f) Inexperienced Drivers*

cc	None	1	2	3
0-50	0	0	0	0
51+	0	10	20	30

(g) No Claim Discount

No Claim Discount			
Nil	1 yr	2 yrs	3 yrs
11	7	4	0

(h) Excess Value – Comprehensive & T.P.F. & T. covers only

1 point to be added for each £100 or part thereof in excess of £1,500.

NET POINTS TOTAL

** NET PREMIUM

**The premium is subject to confirmation from the Regional Office.

Gross Premium _____ (RO Use)

*An inexperienced driver is one who holds a provisional licence or has not held a full UK licence for at least 12 months.

DRIVING

6. Will the motor cycle be driven

(a) solely by you? YES ☐ NO ☐ If 'YES' to (a) the insurance will restrict driving to yourself.

(b) solely by you and your employees? YES ☐ NO ☐ If 'YES' to (b) or (c) complete the following table in respect of all other persons who will drive.

(c) by any other persons? YES ☐ NO ☐ Driving will then be restricted to yourself and to the persons named.

Full name	Age	No. of accidents in last 3 years	Occupation(s) (including part time)	Is a current UK licence to drive a motor cycle held?		Has a full UK licence been held for at least one year?	
(1)				YES	NO	YES	NO
(2)				YES	NO	YES	NO
(3)				YES	NO	YES	NO

7. Have you or has any person who will drive the motor cycle

If 'YES' give full details including the dates of and penalties imposed following a conviction for a motor offence

(a) been convicted of any offence, other than parking, in connection with ANY Motor Vehicle or is such prosecution pending? YES ☐ NO ☐ _____

(b) any physical handicap or infirmity? YES ☐ NO ☐ _____

(c) ever been refused renewal of a motor insurance or has any company or underwriter declined or cancelled the insurance of any motor vehicle or imposed special terms? YES ☐ NO ☐ _____

NO CLAIM DISCOUNT

8. Are you entitled to a 'No Claim Discount' from your previous insurers? YES ☐ NO ☐ If 'YES' attach last renewal notice

9. Have you held any previous motor insurance with this Company? YES ☐ NO ☐ If 'YES' please state policy number(s) and expiry date(s)

PREMIUM PAYMENT BY INSTALMENTS

10. If you qualify do you wish to pay the premium by quarterly instalments? (See note overleaf for details.) YES ☐ NO ☐

DECLARATION

I hereby declare that:—

(a) the motor cycle to be insured is in good and roadworthy condition and has not been modified, altered or adapted in any way from the manufacturer's design.

(b) I have not suppressed, misrepresented or misstated any material fact. (See Definition of Material Facts below.)

(c) all the above statements and particulars, which I have read over and checked, are true to the best of my knowledge and belief.

I hereby apply for a contract of insurance between PEARL ASSURANCE PUBLIC LIMITED COMPANY and myself and agree to pay the premium thereon. The proposal and declaration shall be the basis of the contract of insurance (and any renewal thereof which may be agreed) and I agree to accept the policy, subject to the terms, conditions and conditions expressed therein.

Proposer's Signature _____ Date _____

IMPORTANT: A CERTIFICATE OF INSURANCE OR A COVER NOTE EMBODYING A CERTIFICATE OF INSURANCE MUST BE IN FORCE BEFORE A MOTOR CYCLE IS TAKEN ON THE ROAD.

The liability of the Company does not commence until this proposal has been accepted by the Company, except as provided by any official cover note issued by the Company.

DEFINITION OF MATERIAL FACTS: Material facts are those which an insurer would regard as likely to influence acceptance or assessment of the risk proposed. If in any doubt whether a fact is material or not it must be disclosed. FAILURE TO FULLY DISCLOSE A MATERIAL FACT COULD INVALIDATE THE INSURANCE.

Agents

Agents are employed by insurance companies to "sell" insurance. They know all about the various policies of their company. Some agents will call regularly to collect premiums, and they will suggest to people what might be covered. Agents get commission on the value of insurance cover signed up. Bank managers, accountants, solicitors or others who advise people on money matters are often **part-time** agents for one or two companies. They receive commission on policies arranged.

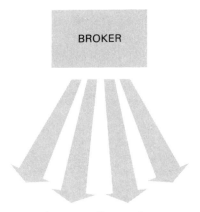

Brokers

Brokers are independent of any company. They are professional experts in insurance, who will advise clients in their best interest on what and how to insure and with whom. This service is generally free to clients, as most insurance companies will pay commission on business placed with them.

Q1 What are the four P's of insurance? Explain each.

Q2 In a Proposal Form covering fire risk on a house, the question would be asked as to what material the roof was made of. Why do you think a higher premium would be charged for a thatched roof than for a slate roof?

Q3 What other questions do you think might be asked on a Proposal Form covering fire risk on a house?

Q4 You are a young office worker sharing a furnished flat. You will wish to insure your guitar and the stereo equipment you have been building up over months.
  a) What risks would you wish to cover?
  b) What questions do you think might be included on the Proposal Form to enable the insurance company to assess the risk?

Q5 What is the difference between an insurance broker and an insurance agent?

Section 3

Principles of insurance

Certain rules apply to all insurance policies. If these rules are not obeyed, the policy may prove to be useless.

Utmost Good Faith

Mr Watson completed a proposal form for a life policy. One of the questions asked on the form was "Have you ever had heart trouble?" He had had a minor heart attack the previous year, but did not admit it on the form. Three years later he in fact died of heart failure; and his widow expected to receive £5,000 benefit on his life policy. However, the true facts came to light when enquiries were made by the insurance company and they refused to pay out.

Mr. Howard took out an insurance policy on his car. The premium charged by the insurance company will depend on several factors. One of the questions asked on the proposal form was whether the car was kept in a garage at night. Mr Howard wrote "Yes"; but in fact every night he left it parked in the road ready for the next day. Five years later the car was stolen at night. The insurance company, after enquiring into the theft, refused to pay the full compensation. They said that a higher premium should have been paid in the circumstances and, therefore, the full value of the loss was not covered.

The principle of **utmost good faith** means that any fact will be made known or revealed that might affect assessment of the risk, for the contract of insurance to stand.

Insurable Interest

The principle of **insurable interest** states that you may only take out insurance where you yourself stand to lose financially, e.g. on your own possessions, your leather coat, your car, your house. The extent of your "insurable interest" is the amount you stand to lose.

With a life policy you may insure your own life or that of the person you are married to. You may only insure the life or the property of some other person if you stand to lose money directly by their loss.

Jill is living in her Aunt's house, rent free. When her Aunt dies the house passes to her son and Jill will have to move and will lose financially. She thus has an insurable interest in her Aunt's life, and in the house, against loss by fire, for example.

Indemnity

The principle of **indemnity** states that insurance is intended to replace the value lost. A profit must not be made from an insurance claim: otherwise there might be a "convenient" accident arranged when someone wanted to replace an old possession. Also, you must not receive full compensation from two insurance companies.

Q1 a) What is the principle of Utmost Good Faith?

b) What may happen if this is ignored?

Q2 List three items in which you have an insurable interest.

Q3 a) What is considered an insurable interest for a life policy?

b) Stephen Matthews has a child, Mary, aged four. Has he an insurable interest in her life? Stephen supports his old mother who lives in the top flat of his house. Can his mother insure his life? Explain both answers.

Q4 Which principle of insurance guards against people overclaiming for goods lost?

Q5 Imagine that you are an insurance company, and that John Jones approaches you to insure a Jaguar car. Suggest three questions that you might ask on the proposal form, to illustrate the three principles of insurance. In each case state which principle of insurance you are illustrating.

By paying a higher premium, a "New for Old" policy may be arranged. Under this claims are settled for the cost of replacing an article damaged or lost, at current prices—provided the value insured has been raised in line with rising prices!

Section 4

What can be insured?

What do people want to insure? For what risks do they seek cover?

Property

Property here means any goods which you own, e.g. your car, your transistor radio, your house, your personal possessions. These goods might be damaged, destroyed or stolen.

Prices rise year by year so you must remember to raise the value insured each year. If your house burned down and the value covered was only the same as 10 years ago, you would be thoroughly underinsured.

The Person

People may wish to insure against injury, sickness or death. Your income might then be reduced, or cut off, and your family suffer as a result.

It is not possible to buy another limb or life, like replacing a broken television set; so a scale of payments is set according to the injury e.g. so much for loss of a leg, so much for loss of an eye. If you cannot work as a result of your injury a sum will be paid each week for a fixed number of months. This system operates for policies covering accidents in the home, and holiday insurance.

With life policies each person decides how much benefit they want to "buy", or can afford in premium payments.

Liability

If you are responsible for injury or loss to someone else they may be able to claim off you. If, for instance, your carelessness caused a car accident you might be sued in a court for **damages**, i.e. compensation. If someone were permanently injured they might be awarded a pension for life which you would have to pay. However, if you are covered by liability insurance the insurance company would pay on your behalf up to an agreed amount.

Interest

You are only allowed to insure against risks where you directly stand to lose financially. In most cases this means your own property. The amount you might lose is the extent of your "interest".

However, in some circumstances you might suffer financially through the loss of someone else's property. For example, your uncle allows your brother to use his shed for car repairs on condition that he insures it against fire. Your brother has an insurable interest in the shed through his repair business, even though it belongs to your uncle. Both stand to lose financially.

Q1 What are the four headings under which people seek insurance cover?

Q2 What property might be covered by a holiday insurance policy? Give three examples.

Q3 More people are injured by accidents in the home than on the roads. Give three common causes of home accidents to the person.

Q4 A person is responsible for damage done by their children or animals to neighbours' property. Write down two examples of circumstances where claims might be made. Under which heading above would such risks be insured?

Q5 You rent a television set and although the company is responsible for any day-to-day repairs necessary, you would be responsible for the cost of any damage to, or theft of, the set. Explain whether you have an insurable interest in your rented television set.

Section 5

Common insurances

We are all under risk in our everyday lives.

Personal accident
This insurance provides compensation if somebody is injured or unable to work. There is a fixed scale of payment for the loss of a limb, an eye, or a life. If someone is off work as the result of some accident, a regular sum is paid for so many weeks, e.g. £10 a week.

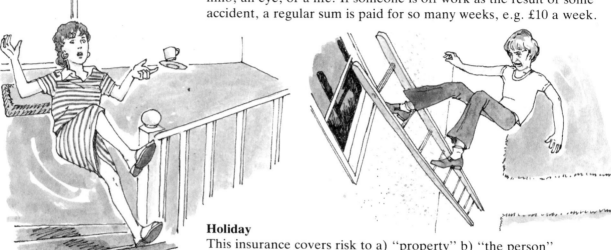

Holiday
This insurance covers risk to a) "property" b) "the person" c) financial "interest".

You may have to cancel your holiday when your tickets and hotel have already been booked and paid for. **"Risk of cancellation"** covers your possible financial loss.

You might have to pay medical expenses abroad.

Q1 Under which of the three types of risk above would you place Risk of Cancellation?

Q2 Give three risks to your person that might arise on holiday.

Q3 a) How would the amount of indemnity be decided for loss of property?
b) How would the amount of compensation be decided for personal accident?

Vehicle

This insurance covers a) property b) the person c) liability.

Q4 Give three or more risks to your property that might be covered by car insurance.

Very often someone other than the car owner is involved in a road accident. The driver may be responsible and liable to pay compensation. This could be for a very large amount: the insurance company will cover this risk.

Road accidents are so widespread, and affect so many families, that this cover for people has been made compulsory by Act of Parliament. The insurance company (1st party) covers the insured person (2nd party) for any accident involving another person (3rd party). This makes sure that money is always available to help people who are injured.

"Act Only" insurance.

Cover for accidents to other people must be held for any vehicle. Anyone driving a car without this cover is breaking the law, and robbing other people of possible compensation.

"Third Party" cover

This insurance consists of Act Only plus damage to other's property, e.g. the cost of repairing another car involved in an accident.

"Third Party Fire and Theft"

This is the minimum cover most car owners choose, covering third party liability plus compensation to the insured for fire or theft of the vehicle.

"Comprehensive" car insurance

Comprehensive insurance includes Third Party, Fire and Theft, accidental damage to your car, things stolen from your car and various other risks.

The amount of premium varies according to the size and make of car; the age and experience of the driver; the place and type of use (business or pleasure).

"No-claims bonus"

This is a reduction in premium as a reward for no claim over a period.

Q5 What vehicle cover is compulsory by law? What is the minimum cover most people choose?

Q6 Explain in your own words a no-claims bonus.

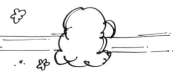

Section 6

Household insurance

The householder would want to insure a) the **structure** of the house itself, the roof, walls etc; b) his possessions inside the house i.e. the **contents**.

Q1 Give four risks that the structure and contents might be insured against.

Q2 What three questions might be asked in the proposal form, in order that the insurance company can assess various risks?

Q3 a) List five items in the house below which you would want covered by contents insurance.

b) Taking the kitchen alone, estimate the total cost of replacing the cooker, the refrigerator and the washing machine.

Under a householder's policy "contents" may be covered only when in the house but you might want to add insurance protection for certain possessions outside the house.

Q4 Give five examples of possessions often taken outside the house for which you might want extra cover.

The householder has a duty to provide safe premises for visitors. If the householder is responsible for injuries to others, or damage to someone else's property, he may have to pay out. Liability insurance will protect the family from this risk.

Q5 Give five examples where a claim might be made against a householder.

Insurance companies offer "package policies" covering a variety of risks, to suit the ordinary person. A **householder's** package policy will cover structure, contents, liability and sometimes personal accident. Some insurance companies call package policies "Comprehensive" or "All Risks". Don't let this mislead you! In fact a policy only covers the risks mentioned in the small print. Nearly all householder's policies do not cover television sets, or jewellery, or cash-on-the-premises above a certain sum; and many leave out mirrors and basins, and do not pay claims under £15. Additional cover has to be arranged for these.

Q6 Why might insurance policies called Comprehensive or All Risks be misleading?

Q7 a) If the premium for a Householder's policy is 20p a year per £100 of cover, what would be the yearly premium for £20,000 cover?

b) The household asks the insurance company to add to the policy £300 protection for a rented colour television set. At 40p per £100 of cover, how much extra premium would the householder have to pay?

If you suffer loss, you should notify the insurance company immediately, and they will send you a claim form to complete. They may wish to check the facts or the amount of your claim.

Q8 Give three questions that you might have to answer on a burglary claim form.

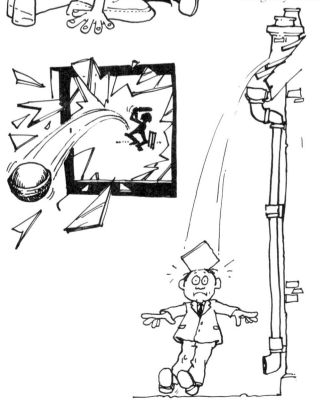

PEARL ASSURANCE PUBLIC LIMITED COMPANY			FOR DISTRICT OFFICE USE ONLY		

FIRE CLAIM FORM
FOR HOUSEHOLD GOODS NOT EXCEEDING £25

Policy No. _____ / _____

1. Full name and address. (BLOCK LETTERS)
2. Fully describe the cause of the fire.
3. State the date and time of the damage.

A full list of the articles damaged or destroyed to be inserted below:—

Description of damaged or destroyed article	Date of purchase or presentation £	Present day price of article £	Deduction for wear and tear £	Value of the salvage £	Net amount claimed after deduction of such salvage and allowance for wear and tear £
				TOTAL £	

*Codes 13, 14 & 38 policies — No deduction to be made except in the case of clothing or household linen or articles more than three years old.

I declare that

(a) the damaged articles belong to me or to members of my family permanently residing with me,

(b) there are no other insurances covering the damaged property and

(c) the statements made are true in every respect.

Date _____   Signature _____

IMPORTANT

DOES YOUR SUM INSURED REFLECT THE FULL VALUE OF YOUR HOUSEHOLD GOODS?

IF NOT AND THIS HAD BEEN A MORE SUBSTANTIAL CLAIM, YOU COULD HAVE FACED HAVING TO MEET A PROPORTION OF THE CLAIM YOURSELF.

TO INCREASE YOUR SUM INSURED, PLEASE COMPLETE THE OTHER SIDE OF THIS SLIP.

Section 7

Business policies

Q1 For what risks do you think a manufacturing company would want insurance cover?

Q2 For what risks do you think a shop would want insurance cover?

A fire may interrupt a profitable business. The loss is greater than the damage caused to the premises, because although business is interrupted expenses continue, such as wages. Alternate premises may have to be rented for stock etc. Fire insurance can be extended to **Consequential loss**. This provides a sum necessary to pay expenses for the period until the business is working again. Premiums are based on statistics on the overall claims likely to arise from Consequential loss.

Q3 What is meant by Consequential loss?

A business may wish to insure against the possible dishonesty of a particular employee who handles large sums of money for the company, e.g. a wages clerk. The insurance company may investigate the individual's background before agreeing a **Fidelity Guarantee** policy.

Q4 What is a Fidelity Guarantee policy? What questions might the insurance company ask about a person to be covered by this type of policy?

There are three types of risk where a business might have to pay compensation to others, and so would seek **Liability** insurance.

Employer's liability
The employer is responsible for providing safe working conditions. Compensation may have to be paid to an employee injured at work. The law makes this type of insurance compulsory on employers, so that any injured employee can be sure that money is available to pay compensation.

Product liability
A supplier may have to pay compensation to anyone who is injured by a faulty product of his. The business may insure against such claims by purchasers.

Public liability
A business must provide safe conditions for anyone coming on the premises. They insure against compensation which might have to be paid to customers or visitors receiving injury.

Q5 List the three types of liability for which a business might take out insurance. Give examples under each heading of situations that might arise in a hairdressing business.

The risk a business cannot insure against is decline of profits. This may be caused by inefficiency; rising costs; out-of-date stock; shoplifting; changing fashion; a bad season; or a national crisis. Business profit may also depend on how hard a man works. Because it is impossible for the insurance company to calculate these things, profit is an uninsurable risk.

Q6 Explain in your own words why business profits are uninsurable.
Q7 Imagine three businesses in circumstances where their profits decline. Write a paragraph on each. Would there be an insurable risk in any of these circumstances?

Section 8

Lloyd's of London

In the eighteenth century coffee drinking became very fashionable and coffee houses were a regular meeting place for men. The coffee house opened by Edward Lloyd in 1688 in the City of London was conveniently near the port of London, and became a meeting place for captains and merchants. Men organising trading voyages would get others to **underwrite** the risk of loss at sea, of the vessel or its cargo. In return for a payment in advance the underwriter guaranteed to pay out to cover the cost of any loss. The traders could expand their overseas activities with some confidence, and the underwriters also gained financially.

Edward Lloyd began to collect and put up information on ships' progress and to provide a news service to help this business of marine insurance. It developed rapidly in size and importance and transferred to larger, and still larger premises. Though the coffee house has long since vanished, the name remains. **Lloyd's of London** is the leading insurance market in the world. From marine insurance of **hull and cargo**, they have expanded to cover all types of insurance all over the world. This insurance market is now housed in a great modern building in the City of London.

Edward Lloyd's Coffee House

The Dealing Room at Lloyd's of London

Q1 How did the name Lloyd's come to be linked with insurance?

Q2 How did marine insurance help the growth of Britain's trade?

Q3 What is meant by "hull" and "cargo" — the two aspects of marine insurance?

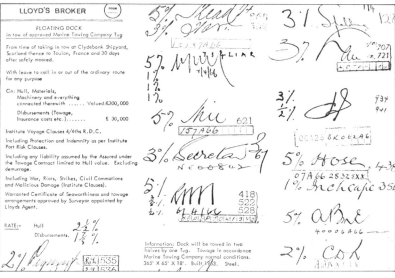

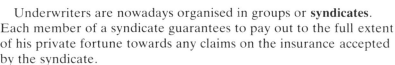

The Slip

Underwriters are nowadays organised in groups or **syndicates**. Each member of a syndicate guarantees to pay out to the full extent of his private fortune towards any claims on the insurance accepted by the syndicate.

Only members of Lloyd's are allowed to do business there. Members are of two main types, **underwriters** and **brokers**. Brokers at Lloyd's represent clients who wish to have insurance, e.g. on a new oil tanker. The broker will write the total value to be covered on a **Slip**, and take this round to different syndicates, who may each accept a part of the risk, e.g. £1,000,000 (4%) towards a total of £25,000,000. The underwriter's agent initials the amount accepted on behalf of the syndicate, and later a proper contract or policy is drawn up.

Q4 What is an underwriter?

Q5 What is a broker at Lloyd's?

Q6 What is a "Slip"?

The world wide reputation of Lloyd's was built up in the last century. £100 m. was paid out promptly after the San Francisco earthquake of 1906 when fire swept through half the city.

Lloyd's underwriters may use judgement rather than statistics as a basis for the risks they are prepared to cover, and the premiums they charge. They cover a far wider range of risks than insurance companies, particularly of new and large undertakings. The risks covered have grown steadily with modern technical progress.

Q7 Look at the pictures on the left. Give five modern undertakings requiring enormous sums of money for which insurance cover may be sought at Lloyd's

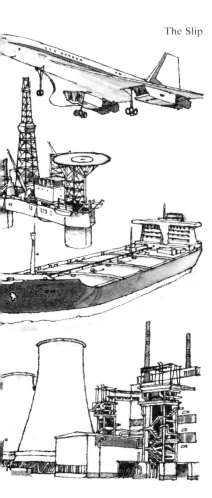

Section 9

Life insurance

If a person has life insurance, this means that a sum of money will be paid out when he dies. He himself cannot get the benefit, of course, so the premiums paid are to provide financial protection for his family.

Most holiday insurance policies include a promise to pay a sum if the person dies on holiday. A holiday policy is arranged for a fixed period or **term**. This type of policy is called a **Term policy**. However, when somebody talks about life insurance he generally thinks of something lasting for a longer time than a holiday. With a **Whole-Life policy** a person may be paying premiums for a large part of his whole life. This is the same as saving throughout life for his family. But with life insurance, the policy comes into force immediately the first premium has been paid: so if someone died in an accident only a month or two after the policy started, his family would still get the full amount promised.

Q1 Jimmy Brown takes out a Term policy to cover his holiday in Spain. The term is one month from 1st August. Is the benefit paid out
   a) if he dies on 10th August from meeting a shark whilst out swimming?
   b) if he dies in a motor cycle accident on 5th September?

Q2 Jack Bannister takes out a Whole-Life policy when he gets married at the age of 25, for £10,000. His premium is £4 a month or £48 a year. How much will be paid out
   a) if he dies at the age of 27 after falling off a ladder?
   b) if he dies at the age of 75 from an infection?

Life insurance is based on statistics of births and deaths that have been collected over 150 years. **Actuaries** are mathematicians who study these figures to calculate the average length of life, and for how long someone is likely to pay premiums before she dies.

Look at the diagram at the top of the next page.
Q3 By how many years did the average life span increase for both men and women between 1871 and 1981? Give three reasons for this improvement.
Q4 At the age of 20, how much longer can you expect to live?

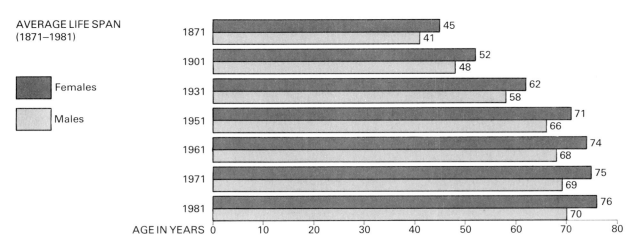

AVERAGE LIFE SPAN (1871–1981)

Females
Males

AGE IN YEARS

Year	Females	Males
1871	45	41
1901	52	48
1931	62	58
1951	71	66
1961	74	68
1971	75	69
1981	76	70

After paying premiums for many years, someone might like to enjoy the benefit herself while she is still alive. With an **Endowment** policy she can arrange for the benefit to be paid at a date fixed, e.g. retiring age. If she dies before the date fixed, her family still receives the full benefit.

Q5 Why do you think that many people chose retiring age for payment of the benefit under an endowment policy?

Q6 A grandmother takes out an endowment policy on her own life to be a present for her new baby granddaughter. At what age do you think the benefit would make a lovely present for the girl?

With life policies premiums are generally paid into a fund over a great number of years. The money does not lie idle. The insurance company invests the money in industry and business, and the interest and dividends return to swell the fund. This means that the insurance companies can promise benefits on a policy larger than the total of premiums paid in, so that the insured person is sharing the advantage of the investments.

Q7 Copy the diagram below.

Q8 What payments are flowing into the fund; and what payments are made from the fund?

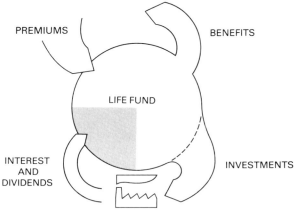

PREMIUMS

BENEFITS

LIFE FUND

INTEREST AND DIVIDENDS

INVESTMENTS

Section 10

Choosing Life Cover

With a life policy a **level premium** is fixed, i.e. the same premium throughout the years (because people generally have less income in old age although there is a higher risk of death).

For each Life Office or company, actuaries decide how much benefit can be **guaranteed** against a premium. Actuaries always allow a margin of safety or surplus in their calculations, in case of unforeseen circumstance, e.g. an epidemic, leading to an exceptional number of deaths in a year. By law, a fund must be revalued every one to three years, to see the exact position, taking into account the number of deaths, the rise and fall of investments, and general expenses. The actual size of the surplus can then be seen for the period past. From the surplus, bonuses are given to policy holders if they hold a **With-Profits** policy. This is slightly more expensive than a without-profits policy, but the bonuses increase the benefit guaranteed, to make these policies a good "buy".

Q1 Why is a level premium fixed for life cover though the risk increases with old age?

Q2 What is meant by a With-Profits policy?

Q3 Why is a With-Profits policy likely to be better value for money?

People generally start thinking about life insurance when they have dependents they want to protect, e.g. children. A young parent has many expenses and will want the highest benefit possible for a low premium. This would be a Term policy, e.g. for 25 years to cover the term of a mortgage. Life offices can guarantee high benefits here as they generally don't have to pay out within the term.

As people become better off they may choose Whole Life cover, to be assured of a payment on death, whenever that is. An Endowment policy is more expensive as it is generally paid out earlier than death; but a man or woman can then enjoy the benefit with their family. If they can afford it, With-Profits endowment or Whole Life policies would be chosen.

Q4 Outline three possible changes in a person's life and income, and link each with a type of life policy.

Insurance funds

Insurance funds, particularly life funds, have grown enormously over the last 25 years. As people have become better off, more can afford to buy protection. Insurance funds are invested in industry and commerce: and these funds are an important source for business expansion.

Advantage of Insurance

Insurance can now be seen as providing four great advantages:
1) it provides protection for people and for property
2) it provides funds which are available to help the growth of industry and commerce
3) it gives businesses the confidence to expand knowing that the risks of loss are spread among many and need not be disastrous for the unfortunate few
4) it benefits Britain by the amount of foreign currency earned from selling insurance overseas. Lloyd's of London is a great world insurance market, and two-thirds of the business arranged there is for the insurance of property in other countries e.g. port installations. Premiums paid from abroad earn foreign currency for Britain, as do exports of goods. Foreign currency earned for services, such as insurance, are known as **invisible exports**.

Q1 Why have insurance funds increased considerably over the past 25 years?

Q2 How are insurance funds put to work?

Q3 Describe the four ways in which insurance benefits the country.

Q4 What premiums could be described as invisible exports?

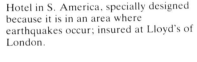

Hotel in S. America, specially designed because it is in an area where earthquakes occur; insured at Lloyd's of London.

Section 11

National insurance

National Insurance is paid by every employed person over school-leaving age who earns over £35.50 a week. This entitles each to receive benefits in the event of unemployment, sickness, industrial injury etc. This protection has been made compulsory by law, and the government runs the scheme. Each person is given a National Insurance number.

NATIONAL INSURANCE NUMBER CARD

Your National Insurance number is:

TN 06 05 66 F

Please show this number to your employer, if he asks for it, and quote it in all communications with DHSS (see Notes overleaf).

MR/MRS/MISS*   *NORMAN*   FORENAME(S)

OLYMP.   SURNAME

9. RUSH ROAD   FULL

NOMAD.   POSTAL ADDRESS

Postcode

*Delete as appropriate

Form CF 354

Issued by the Department of Health and Social Security

The National Insurance contribution is paid partly by the employee, and partly by the employer. The employer's share is the larger. The employee's share is deducted from his/her pay, and the employers are responsible for paying the full contributions, their own and their employee's, to the Collector of Taxes every month. The size of the contribution will vary according to the amount over £35.50 earned in a week. If someone is self-employed or non-employed different contributions and lower benefits may apply.

A certain number of National Insurance contributions entitle people to various benefits. These include:

Unemployment benefit	For those out of work.
Sickness benefit	For those sick and unable to work.
Industrial Injury benefit	For those injured and off work as the result of an accident at work, or through certain industrial diseases.
Death Grant	A sum to help with funeral expenses.
Widow's Benefit	An allowance for the first half-year of widowhood, and weekly payments afterwards depending on circumstances.

Maternity Grant	A sum to help with the expenses of having a baby.
Maternity Allowance	A weekly payment covering a maximum period of 18 weeks some before and some after the birth.
Retirement Pension	Available at 65 for men and 60 for women.
National Health Service	National Insurance contributions go towards providing medical services for everyone.

Q1 Who pays National Insurance contributions?

Q2 List five National Insurance benefits.

Q3 Why has National Insurance made cover against certain risks compulsory for employees?

Q4 Imagine three different sets of circumstances that might arise for you in the next five years, for which National Insurance benefits might be claimed. Write a paragraph on each.

We would now think it quite wrong to allow people in our community to die of starvation in the streets as they do in some poorer parts of the world. Our social conscience has grown in the last 100 years, as Britain has become richer. We now have a Welfare State, which provides a health service, housing and education which many would not be able to pay for privately. Supplementary benefits are made when national insurance benefits or pensions are not enough to meet needs, or are not available.

Q5 What change has the last century seen in the attitude of our community towards want and poverty?

Q6 What is meant by the Welfare State?

Vocabulary

Actuaries
Life insurance mathematicians who calculate probable lengths of life.

Agents
They sell insurance business for a particular company, on commission.

Brokers
Independent professional experts in insurance who advise clients on all companies and policies.

Cancellation risk
The chance of losing the sum you have paid to a travel agent for your holiday, if at the last moment you are unable to go.

Comprehensive insurance
A package policy covering a number of risks.

Compulsory insurance
Insurance which must be held by law.

Consequential loss
Additional financial loss following an accident insured e.g. extra expenses arising after a fire.

Damages
Compensation claimed in a law court e.g. for an accident caused by someone else.

Endowment policy
A policy paying out benefit on an agreed date or at death, if earlier.

Fidelity Guarantee
Insurance covering the honesty of an employee. Fidelity means faithfulness.

Hull and Cargo
The frame or body of a ship, the vessel itself; and the goods carried.

Indemnity
The principle that states that insurance is intended to replace the value lost only.

Insurable interest
The principle of insurance that states that someone may only take out insurance where he/she stands to lose financially.

Invisible exports
Services earning foreign currency for Britain.

Level premium
The same premium paid throughout a policy.

Liability
Responsibility for injury or loss to someone else.

Premiums
Payments in return for insurance cover.

Policy
The contract between the insurance company and the insured person for payment of premiums in return for compensation in the event of loss or damage.

Property
Any goods which you own.

Proposal form
An application for insurance cover, completed with full details of the risk to be covered e.g. vehicle, make, age.

Protection
Insurance against various risks causing financial loss.

Structure
The building itself e.g. walls, roof, pipes etc.

Syndicates
Groups of underwriters.

Term policy
A life policy that lasts for a certain period only e.g. one month.

Underwrite
To promise to pay compensation in the event of loss, in return for a premium.

Uninsurable risks
Where an insurance company is unable to judge the extent of likely claims e.g. shoplifting, it may refuse to provide an insurance policy.

Utmost good faith
The principle of insurance that states that the full truth must be revealed in answers to questions on a proposal form.

Whole Life
A policy whereby premiums are paid throughout someone's life; and benefit is paid on her death to her heirs.

7 Ownership

In Britain, about half of all trading is in private hands, and is run for profit. This is called **private enterprise**. It covers not only the small business owned and perhaps operated by one man, but factories employing thousands; nationally-known shops with hundreds of branches; and giant multi-national companies with bases in several countries.

The other half is owned by the State and run for the benefit of the nation. This is known as **public enterprise**. It covers the production and sale of goods and services by nationalised industries e.g. postal services, broadcasting, electricity, railways.

Sections
1. Owning your own business   Sole traders   Unlimited liability
2. Partners   Partners' Liability
3. Partnership law   The advantages of the limited liability company
4. How a company is run   The Annual General Meeting
5. Company registration
6. Private limited companies   Public limited companies   Private enterprise
7. Shares
8. The Stock Exchange   Stocks
9. Mergers, takeovers and economies of scale   Multinational companies
10. Co-operatives
11. Public enterprise

Section 1   Owning your own business

After working six years in a hairdressing shop, Janet Clegg felt that she knew the business thoroughly. She dreamed of starting up on her own. She wanted to be her own boss, to organise the shop the way she thought best — and to pocket the profits!

John Pelham worked in an engineering factory. His health was not good and the doctor suggested that he should do lighter work. He decided to buy a small shop where he could get help, if necessary, from his wife and children.

Mary Denbow was left £10,000. She decided to take shop premises that had just become vacant on her council estate, to start a launderette. A friend with experience was willing to work with her; and she would be on hand when the children returned home from school.

Trevor Potts inherited his father's antique shop. He had grown up interested in antiques and continued to run the business — though he did not like the long hours and Saturday working.

Susan Bulmer lived on a farm near a charming village visited by tourists. She decided to convert an empty barn and to sell "Farmhouse Teas", using the farm produce.

Martin Nye enjoyed tinkering with engines. He did not like being told what to do in an office but was prepared to work hard on his own. He bought secondhand cars and did them up for sale. He decided to do this full time in a rented garage.

Q1 From the stories above pick out eight reasons influencing people to go into business for themselves.

Q2 Tell two stories of people you know (or imagine) who own businesses.

Sole traders

A great many small businesses open up every year — and a great many close down. A builder or garage owner gives customers their bills after the job is completed. Even with plenty of work, if customers delay payment, the owner may not be able to pay his suppliers and may be forced out of business. On the other hand, a business may prosper and grow. People working for themselves generally work harder and longer hours than they would for someone else.

A **Sole Trader** is a one-person owner. A sole trader may have many employees and several branches. The name does not imply a one-person business, but that one person alone owns the business and receives the profits.

Unlimited liability

A sole trader pockets all the profits, and is responsible (or liable) for all the debts. This is called **Unlimited Liability**.

Any sole trader who cannot meet his debts may be taken to the Bankruptcy Court. They will assess how much a person owes against how much he is worth, taking into account not only the sale value of the business and equipment, but his house, car, furniture, etc. No difference is made between home and business possessions and savings, since one grows from the other. Everything he owns may have to be sold to help pay the debts he has run up, leaving only the tools of the trade and £20 worth of bedding and clothes. According to how much is raised, a settlement towards outstanding debts is declared by the court.

EXAMPLE: J. White has debts of £50,000. The auction of his business and private possessions raises £25,000 or half the debt. The court declares a settlement of 50p in the pound.

Once declared bankrupt, a person may not obtain any credit above £10 without admitting this. If, and when, all the debts are cleared, he is discharged by the court.

Q3 What is a sole trader?

Q4 What is meant by unlimited liability?

Q5 What does it mean to be declared bankrupt?

Q6 How can someone become a discharged bankrupt?

Q7 List three disadvantages of being a sole trader.

Section 2   Partners

Several people working together for profit are called **partners.** They are joint **owners** (not employees).

Joe Simpson runs a successful greengrocery business. As he grows older he needs a younger man to help him with the heavy work, shifting sacks of potatoes etc, and perhaps to take over the daily 5 a.m. trip to Covent Garden. He has employees: but he decides to make his son-in-law Ron an **Active Partner** in the business. This would keep the business in the family when Joe retires, and the young couple would inherit the firm.

Malcolm Maxwell runs a prosperous small firm which makes architectural models. While he handles the selling side of the work, he now relies heavily on Jack's model-making skill, which has developed since he took him on as a school leaver with examination passes in art and mathematics. Jack might seek higher wages elsewhere; so Mr Maxwell decides to offer him a junior partnership. This would give him a share of the profits, an incentive to work hard and loyalty to the business.

Martin Nye is making a success of car renovation. He has a chance of moving into larger premises, and is confident of being able to extend his business. He would also like to maintain some hire cars if he had more money (capital) to buy them. His father agrees to give him several thousand pounds and become a **Sleeping Partner** in the business i.e. having a share of profits, but not taking an active part in its running.

Q1 Give three reasons why a sole trader might want to take a partner.

Q2 Give two advantages to someone being offered a partnership.

Q3 Write two stories of half a page each describing the circumstances in which a partnership may be set up.

Q4 What is the title given to
    a) a partner who takes part in the day-to-day running of the business
    b) a partner who has contributed money but does not take an active part in the business?

Partners' Liability

Partners, like sole traders, have Unlimited Liability. They are responsible or liable for the debts of the business to the full extent of their private fortunes, both jointly and individually. If one partner is less wealthy than another, he may only be able to contribute a lower share, in the event of bankruptcy, towards paying suppliers, and the other partners will have to pay more.

A Partnership is a legally binding relationship. It is extremely important that partners agree and can trust each other, since the business debts run up by one partner are the responsibility of all. A partnership can be formed very easily, often by a spoken agreement only. However, it is wise to have a **Partnership Deed** or legal agreement drawn up, outlining the rights and duties of each partner, to suit their particular circumstances.

Joe Simpson, the greengrocer, built up his business for years before Ron joined him as a partner. He deserves a larger percentage of the profits: but Ron also wants a regular wage. The Partnership Deed might set out that Joe gets 75 percent of the profits while Ron gets a weekly wage plus 25 percent of the profits.

Mr Maxwell included in his Partnership Deed the hours to be worked and the holiday allowance for each partner.

Martin Nye's Partnership Deed included details on the management of the business (by himself), and the interest to be paid on his father's capital contribution in addition to his percentage share of the profits.

Q5 Give two reasons why particular care should be taken when choosing a business partner.

Q6 What is meant by Unlimited Liability in a partnership?

Q7 What is a Deed of Partnership?

Q8 What items might be included in a Partnership Deed?

Q9 What advantage is gained
    a) by a Partnership from a Sleeping Partner?
    b) by a Sleeping Partner from a Partnership?

Section 3

Partnership law

The Partnership Act governs those partnerships where no Partnership Deed has been drawn up. This lays down that profits shall be divided equally between all partners regardless of what they have contributed; and no allowance is made for any wage to a partner. This may not suit the circumstances of all partnerships.

Limited Partnership

Some people are frightened of putting money into a partnership because of the risk to their private possessions of unlimited liability. It is possible in a Partnership Deed to make provision for a **limited partner**. His liability ends with the money he has put into the business. He cannot lose more than this. Since he does not risk so much, he cannot have the same say in the management of the business; the law says that a limited partner must be a sleeping partner. In any partnership there must be at least one active partner with unlimited liability.

Death of a partner

The death of a partner automatically breaks up or dissolves the partnership. The heirs of the dead partner may not want to leave their share of the money in the business and everything may have to be sold.

Size of partnership

By law partnerships may not have more than 20 partners unless they are formed by professional people (selling "advice") e.g. solicitors.

Q1 Why is it advisable for a partnership to have a legal Deed of Partnership drawn up?

Q2 What is a Limited Partnership?

Q3 What is the effect on a partnership of the death of a partner?

Q4 Which of the following partnership businesses are restricted to 20 partners?
a) window-cleaners
b) restaurants
c) solicitors
d) dry-cleaners
e) antique shops
f) insurance brokers
g) garage repair businesses

Q5 Give two possible disadvantages of a partnership as a form of business ownership.

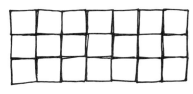

The advantages of the limited liability company

Partnerships are not suitable for the development of giant modern industries. What is needed is:

a) money contributed by a far larger number of people
b) a limit to liability or loss, to give owners confidence that they can invest without risk to their private possessions
c) continuity of the business, regardless of death of an owner.

All these are achieved by the creation of a **Limited Liability Company**.

The money, or "**capital**", required for the business is divided into equal parts or **shares**, which are sold. The buyers, who provide the money required, are called **shareholders** and become the owners of the business. If the business were to fail or "go into liquidation", the shareholders would only lose the money they had paid for their shares, nothing more. Their liability is limited to this.

The Limited Company is registered as an artificial "person" in law, able to conduct business, employ people, make contracts, and be responsible for debts.

Someone may sell his shareholding to others; so the list of shareholders may alter frequently. The Limited Company has a continuing life no matter who are the owners at any time.

Q6 Why are partnerships unsuitable for the development of large scale modern industry?

Q7 What is meant by Limited Liability?

Q8 A large number of people (owners) cannot hope to keep a check on the day-by-day running of a business. Why is limited liability important to shareholders?

Q9 What are three advantages of a Limited Company over a partnership?

Q10 How do you become a part-owner of a limited liability company?

200 YEARS OLD AND STILL GOING STRONG

SHAREHOLDERS · THE COMPANY

Section 4

How a company is run

1 Day-to-day the company is run by managers under the direction of the Managing Director.
2 The policy of the company is formed by the Board of Directors under the leadership of the Chairman of the Board.

   One director at least (i.e. the Managing Director) must be active in the business; but other directors may be knowledgeable outsiders e.g. an MP, an experienced accountant or banker.
3 The Board of Directors has to report once a year to the owners, i.e. the shareholders; who vote on whether they approve the conduct of their company by the Board. They also elect or re-elect directors to the Board.
4 The object of the company is to make a profit. Profit is returned to the shareholder in the form of a **dividend** on shares. For example, a dividend is declared at 15p in the pound. A shareholder of 100 £1 shares gets a dividend that year of £15 (100 × 15p).

Q1 Who is responsible for the day-to-day running of a limited company?
Q2 Who plans the policy of a limited company?
Q3 Who heads and is the spokesman for the Board of Directors?
Q4 To whom is the Board of Directors responsible for the performance of the company?
Q5 How do the owners of the company have a say in its policy?

PEARSON
Annual Report 1985

The Annual General Meeting
At least once a year the shareholders of a limited company must be invited to a meeting to vote on the policy of the company.

   With the advanced notice of the Annual General Meeting (AGM) the printed **Chairman's Report** is sent to shareholders. This reports on and explains the performance of the company during the past

year, and outlines plans for the future.

The **Annual Accounts** of the company are also sent to shareholders, showing the company's financial position and the year's trading figures and profit. The accounts have to be **audited** or certified as correct by an outside firm of accountants. A distribution of profits, or dividend on shares, is recommended. Some of the profit is retained, kept in the company towards new machinery, expansion, etc.

At the AGM the Chairman makes a speech about the company's progress. The accounts are presented by the Financial Director, the Company Accountant or Company Secretary, who answers questions.

The shareholders then vote on whether they accept the report, the accounts, and the dividend. Other policy proposals may also be discussed and voted on. Directors are elected to the Board or stand for re-election every few years.

If a shareholder does not attend the AGM, she may vote by 'proxy'. A proxy form is often sent with the notice of the meeting. The shareholder may sign this to give the Chairman (or another shareholder) the right to vote on her behalf.

One share carries one vote. A block of 100 shares carries 100 votes. A large shareholding may thus control the voting.

Q6 What do shareholders receive with their notice of the Annual General Meeting?

Q7 What does the Chairman's Report cover?

Q8 What do the annual accounts show?

Q9 How may shareholders be confident that the accounts are correct?

Q10 May shareholders only vote if they attend the meeting?

Q11 How may someone gain control of a company?

ERITH & COMPANY LIMITED

FORM OF PROXY FOR ANNUAL GENERAL MEETING

I/We, ...
(BLOCK CAPITALS PLEASE)

of ....
being (a) Member/Members of the above-named Company, hereby appoint the Chairman of the Meeting

or ....
as my/our proxy to vote for me/us and on my/our behalf as indicated below at the Annual General Meeting of the Company to be held on 20th May, 1976 and at any adjournment thereof.

Dated this .... May, 1986

Signature(s) ....

Please indicate how you wish your proxy to vote by placing an **"X"** in the appropriate box. If no indication is given the proxy will vote or abstain as he thinks fit.

	For	Against			For	Against
Ordinary Resolution 1			Ordinary Resolution 3(*a*)			
Ordinary Resolution 2			Ordinary Resolution 3(*b*)			
			Ordinary Resolution 4			

Notes:—
(1) In the case of a Corporation this form should be executed under its Common Seal or under the hand of an officer or attorney duly authorised in writing.
(2) This Form of Proxy and the power of attorney or other authority, if any, under which it is signed, must be lodged not later than twenty-four hours before the time fixed for the holding of the Meeting at the address overleaf or be handed to the Chairman of the Meeting.
(3) If it is desired to appoint as proxy any person other than the Chairman of the Meeting, delete "the Chairman of the Meeting" and insert the name and address of your proxy; the alteration should be initialled.
(4) In the case of joint holders, the vote of the first named holder will be accepted.

Printed by Eden Fisher & Co. Ltd., England   J84987

Section 5

Company registration

A limited company is created by registering the "birth" with the Registrar of Companies. There are a number of laws governing the formation and conduct of limited companies. Two documents must be filed with the Registrar.

1. Memorandum of Association

This gives details of the company as it affects the **external** or outside world, for example:
a) name of the company
b) registered address
c) the scope of its activities (e.g. to manufacture toys): the company must stick within the declared trading objectives
d) the size of the capital to be raised (e.g. £100,000). Only shares up to this amount may be issued
e) the number and face value of the shares (e.g. 100,000 £1 shares).

2. Articles of Association

These give details of the **internal** organisation and the rights of shareholders, for example:
a) arrangements for an AGM to which shareholders must be invited
b) arrangements for audited annual accounts which must be sent to shareholders
c) voting rights of shareholders
d) a Director's length of service before standing for re-election.

A registration fee is charged, according to the size of the registered capital. A **Certificate of Incorporation** is issued by the Registrar of Companies as permission to trade as a limited company.

The word "Limited" must appear in the title of a limited liability company, either Ltd (e.g. Top Toy Co. Ltd.) or PLC, public limited company (e.g. Marks and Spencer PLC).

The limited company must file its annual accounts each year with the Registrar and these are available for viewing by anyone.

Q1 With whom is the birth of a limited company registered?
Q2 a) What document sets out the size and trading aims of a limited company?
  b) Give three other items included in this document.
Q3 a) What document sets out the rights of shareholders?
  b) Give three important aspects of these rights.
Q4 What decides the fee charged for the registration of a limited company?
Q5 How may anyone recognise a limited company?
Q6 What further documents have to be lodged each year with the Registrar of Companies?

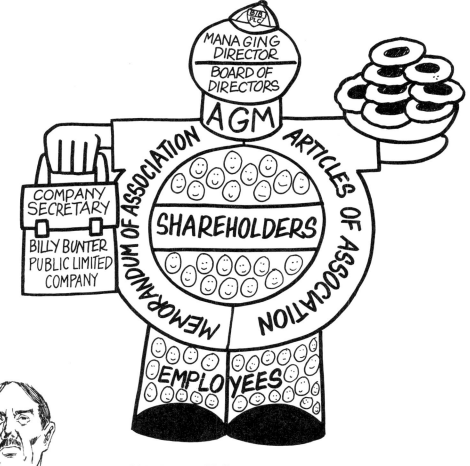

PRODUCTION MANAGER

PURCHASING MANAGER

Billy Bunter PLC
Registered name: Billy Bunter Company PLC

Registered address: Grey Friars School Road

Registered aims: to produce jam tarts.

The company's size is outlined by the Memorandum of Association, and the shareholders are protected by the Articles of Association.

The Board of Directors are at the head of the company and are supported by the AGM.

The Managing Director has on his thinking cap for the organisation and progress of the company.

Only some of the shareholders in fact bother to attend the AGM.

The employees keep the company on the move.

The Company Secretary is the employee in charge of all paperwork and administration.

Q7 Copy the Billy Bunter PLC drawing, taking a full page.
Q8 Who is responsible for company administration and paperwork?
Q9 Name four other possible managers in a large company.

Section 6

There are two types of limited company, Private and Public. Limited liability companies can be formed by two or more shareholders.

Private Limited Company (Ltd)

It is "**Private**" because the shares may only be sold privately and with the agreement of other shareholders. This enables a family to keep control of a company they have built up.

Malcolm Maxwell's architectural models are in great demand as a result of new town planning schemes in his locality. He has more business than he can cope with. He needs more capital for larger premises, more stock, and more workers. He decides to change his business status from a partnership to a Private Limited Company.

He would continue to control the business with a majority shareholding. Jack, his junior partner, would also be a shareholder and sit on the Board of Directors, as well as being an employee. The necessary money for expansion could be raised by selling shares to friends and relatives familiar with the success of the business. All the shareholders would have the protection of limited liability, and, if they wanted ready money, could sell their shares privately, with the agreement of the other shareholders.

Public Limited Company (PLC)

It is called "**Public**" because the company may advertise the sale of shares to the public, and shares may be bought and sold freely on the Stock Exchange.

Arranging for a new issue of shares at the Stock Exchange is costly, so a company will only "go public" when it wants to raise a large sum of money from a wide circle of the public. A Public Limited Company must have at least two shareholders. Public companies come under stricter laws and regulations than private companies, in order to safeguard the interest of widespread shareholders.

Q1 How few shareholders may a Limited Company have?

Q2 Why is a Private Limited Company a suitable form of business ownership for a family business?

Q3 Why might a partnership become a Private Limited Company?

Q4 What is the difference between the meaning of the words "Private" and "Public" in relation to a limited liability company?

Q5 What considerations would influence a private limited company in deciding whether or not to "go public"?

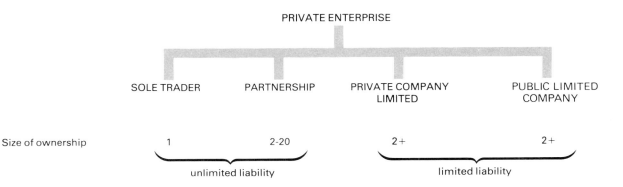

Private enterprise

Private Enterprise is business run to make a profit for its individual owners. It is part of private property. People put money into business in order to get a return in the form of profits or dividends.

Decisions made about business are generally towards increasing profits for the private owners. Business enterprise ranges from the individual working alone, through various sized groupings of owners and employees, to the giant multi-national company operating in several countries.

Anyone can start up in business if he has a good idea of how to make money. In large companies the owners, the shareholders, play little part in the day-to-day running of the business, though the object of the business is to increase their dividends. As company units get larger, the number of owners generally increases, and they are separated from management. More laws and regulations then safeguard the interests of shareholders.

Notice that a Public limited company is part of Private Enterprise.

Q6 What do you understand by Private Enterprise?

Q7 What types of business ownership are included in Private Enterprise?

Q8 What is the object of decisions made in Private Enterprise?

Q9 Why do large private enterprises generally have more owners?

Section 7

Shares

Shareholders put money into a business in order to get a share of the profits. The **dividend** is the yearly distribution of profit to shareholders. Shares are "risk capital" because the dividend depends on trading results during the year.

A dividend is declared as a percentage on the face value of a share. Example, a 5 per cent dividend declared pays 5p on a £1 share. A shareholding of £100 would then get £5. The dividend is generally paid in two parts, e.g. in May and November.

There are a number of different types of share. The most common are:

1. Ordinary shares

These are the main risk-bearing shares, where dividend varies from year to year. They are sometimes called **equity** because each one has an equal share in the ownership of the company's capital.

2. Preference shares

These earn a fixed dividend, e.g. "7% Preference Shares". They get "**preference**" over ordinary shares in that their fixed dividend is paid out before it is decided how much to pay on ordinary shares. Also, if the company were to fail or "**go into liquidation**", and if there were any money left after all debts had been paid, the preference shareholders would get their capital back before ordinary shareholders.

3. Cumulative Preference shares

If the full fixed dividend is not paid out one year to holders of "cumulative" shares, the under-payment is accumulated or carried

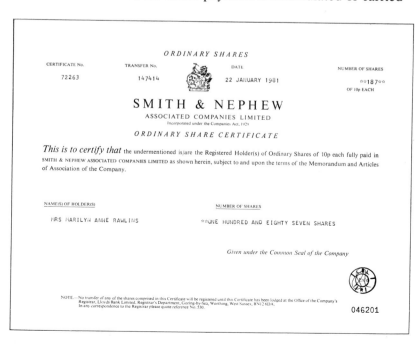

Share certificate

forward to following years. It must then be paid, together with the dividend due for that year, before payment is made to ordinary shareholders.

In a good year of high profits, ordinary shareholders may receive a much higher dividend than preference shareholders. On the other hand, in a poor year preference shareholders may get more than ordinary shareholders. Some people prefer the greater certainty of fixed-dividend preference shares.

Q1 What is a dividend?
Q2 Why is shareholding called "risk capital"?
Q3 In what form are profits distributed to shareholders?
Q4 What are Preference shares?
Q5 Why do Ordinary shares carry more risk than preference shares?
Q6 Why do some people favour preference shares?
Q7 What is a Cumulative Preference share?

Share certificate and dividend voucher

The Share Certificate is proof of ownership, sent to a shareholder when he buys shares in a company. It shows the face value of each share and the number of shares held.

A Dividend Slip is sent half yearly to each shareholder showing the dividend which is being paid. The number of shares held by the shareholder is entered and the total amount due is calculated. Income tax is deducted "at source", i.e. before payment out by the company, (who is responsible for paying the tax to the Inland Revenue department). The remaining amount is the net payment due, for which a cheque is forwarded with the dividend slip.

Q8 Name the Company by whom the Share Certificate opposite was issued and the amount and type of the shareholding.
Q9 What dividend per share was payable in the half-year illustrated below, and how much was paid to the shareholder after deduction of tax "at source"?

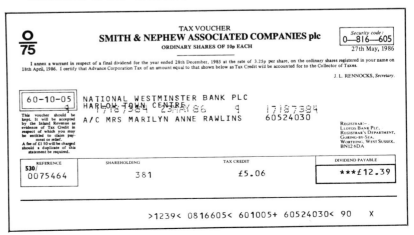

TAX VOUCHER
SMITH & NEPHEW ASSOCIATED COMPANIES plc
ORDINARY SHARES OF 10p EACH

Security code: 0—816—605
27th May, 1986

I annex a warrant in respect of a final dividend for the year ended 28th December, 1985 at the rate of 3.25p per share, on the ordinary shares registered in your name on 18th April, 1986. I certify that Advance Corporation Tax of an amount equal to that shown below as Tax Credit will be accounted for to the Collector of Taxes.

J. L. RENNOCKS, Secretary.

60-10-05

NATIONAL WESTMINSTER BANK PLC
HARLOW TOWN CENTRE
A/C MRS MARILYN ANNE RAWLINS
60524030

This voucher should be kept. It will be accepted by the Inland Revenue as evidence of Tax Credit in respect of which you may be entitled to claim payment or relief.
A fee of £1.50 will be charged should a duplicate of this statement be required.

Registrar:—
Lloyds Bank Plc,
Registrar's Department,
Goring-by-Sea,
Worthing, West Sussex,
BN12 6DA.

REFERENCE	SHAREHOLDING	TAX CREDIT	DIVIDEND PAYABLE
530/ 0075464	381	£5.06	***£12.39

>1239< 0816605< 601005+ 60524030< 90   X

Section 8

The Stock Exchange

The Stock Exchange is a market place where stocks and shares in public limited companies may be bought and sold. Shares are bought **at** the Stock Exchange, not from the Stock Exchange. Only members are allowed to deal in shares on "The Floor".

Members are of two types, market-makers and broker-dealers. **Market-makers** are like wholesalers, buying and holding shares for resale at a profit. They are grouped on the Floor at "pitches" or stands for those specialising in a particular type of share e.g. mining; or retail plcs. **Broker-dealers** act on behalf of clients wishing to buy shares as an investment, or to sell them. The same company may employ both broker-dealers and market-makers, but the two functions are kept separate.

A member of the public wishing to buy or sell shares must do it through a broker-dealer, who will give advice, and charge a percentage commission on deals. The broker-dealer approaches a number of market-makers to ask their prices, without disclosing whether he wishes to buy or sell. Each market-maker quotes two prices, the buying price (lower) and the selling price (higher) e.g. 110 (p) and 112 (p). The broker-dealer then picks the market-maker whose price is most favourable for his client, i.e. the lowest price he can buy for or the highest price he can sell for. After agreeing with the market-maker the number of shares to be traded at the price, each makes a note; and the necessary documents are later drawn up and sent out for signing, and registration of the official transfer of ownership.

The market-maker, immediately the deal is made, feeds the details into the Stock Exchange computer, SEAQ (Stock Exchange Automated Quotations). The computer is also constantly up-dated with the details of other deals being conducted by telephone from broker-dealer's offices, instead of on the Floor. The SEAQ electronic price information system is available nation-wide, showing a complete list of all market-makers, with buying and selling prices. The London Stock Exchange is the largest market for stocks and shares in the world, with world-wide deals.

Q1 What is the Stock Exchange?

Q2 Who are the two types of members of the Stock Exchange?

Q3 a) On whose behalf does a broker-dealer act?
b) How is a broker-dealer paid?

Q4 Why does the market-maker quote two prices for each share?

Q5 How does a broker-dealer obtain the best deal for clients?

Share Movement

If a company is doing well, and declaring high dividends, many people will want to buy its shares. This will lead to a rise in their price. An unfavourable annual report or low dividends may lead shareholders to sell. As more of these shares come on the market, the price will fall.

Market-makers' prices for different shares respond daily, sometimes hourly, to the amount of activity in buying and selling. Daily prices are printed in some newspapers, e.g. the *Financial Times*.

If a share is bought at its face value (i.e. the price of a £1 share is £1), it is easy to calculate the profit, or **yield**; e.g. a 5 per cent dividend yields 5p per £1 share. If, however, £2 has been paid for the share a 5p dividend represents a yield of only 2½ per cent, i.e. half that above.

Q6 What will be the effect on share prices of a profitable year for a company?

Q7 Look at the graph below and find the price of the share on February 1st and on April 15th.

Q8 What is the difference between the highest and lowest share prices in the graph?

BILLY BUNTER PLC SHARE PRICE MOVEMENT 1982

Stocks

On the Stock Exchange trading in **stocks** takes place as well as in shares. Stocks sold raise money for an organisation, but do NOT carry a share of ownership. Their price varies daily, like shares.

Debentures

A **debenture** is a **loan** to a public limited company paying fixed **interest**. The period during which the loan will be repaid is generally shown e.g. "8% Debenture 1990–95".

Government Bonds

Bonds raise money for the government, for nationalised industries or local authorities. Bonds pay fixed interest e.g. "8% Treasury Bonds".

Q9 What is the name given to the payment or "return" on a share?

Q10 Name two types of share and two types of stock that carry a fixed return.

Q11 What is the difference between a share and a debenture?

Section 9

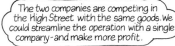

Mergers, takeovers and economies of scale

Companies may **merge** to make one larger company; or a big company may **take over** a smaller one. They hope that by pooling resources and streamlining their organisation, they will make more profit than by competing with each other. They can pool their ideas and techniques, and their lists of customers. The larger a production line, the more goods can be produced in the same time, on one site. These savings on the cost of production are called **economies of scale**. Savings can also be made on administration, i.e. office costs, and on advertising etc.

Mergers may be arranged between two companies in the same line of business e.g. computers. Or a manufacturer may seek retail "outlets", and take over a chain of shops. A successful retail business, on the other hand, may want to merge with a manufacturer of the goods it handles, thus cutting out the wholesale layer, and absorbing the profit. Boots, for example, is a manufacturing–retail pharmacy multiple.

The danger of mergers and takeovers is that fewer and fewer giants dominate a market. If one organisation were to reach a position of **monopoly** where it was alone in dominating a market, either as regards supplies or sales, there would be no competition to keep its prices down and its standards up. To avoid this, the **Monopolies and Mergers Commission** investigates proposed mergers and takeovers. If they are not considered to be in the public interest, they are not allowed.

Q1 What effect do economies of scale have on the costs of producing each item? Explain your answer.

Q2 Explain in your own words what is meant by "economies of scale".

Q3 What is the job of the Monopolies and Mergers Commission?

Q4 Why might a merger or takeover not be allowed?

Multinational companies

Many companies export goods all over the world: but some decide that it would be cheaper to produce their goods overseas, close to their foreign customers. These companies with overseas factories are called **multinational companies**.

Many multinational companies have factories all over the globe, e.g. Ford is an American car assembler which produces cars in Britain, as well as in other European countries, Australasia and South America. Different parts may be manufacturered in half a dozen different countries and taken to another country for assembly. The early British multinational companies were involved in rubber, tea and sugar production in the Commonwealth. More recent British multinationals are concerned with the electrical, chemical and electronic industries.

Multinationals bring jobs to the countries in which they set up production and some of the profits they make are left in the foreign country to re-invest in new machinery and further expansion—though most of the profits are returned to the parent company. Multinationals are now so enormously powerful, with funds bigger than many States, that they can transfer as it suits them. Some multinationals arrange their finances so that they pay little tax in some countries, so depriving that country of valuable revenue. Some less-developed countries are so dependent on multinational companies that if they chose to transfer their factories, severe unemployment and economic problems would result. Some of their large profits are made from the very low wages paid to their workers in less-developed countries, for long hours worked.

Q5 Why do some companies become multinational?

Q6 Name four industries in which multinational companies operate.

Q7 What is the main advantage of multinational companies producing in a country?

Q8 Explain two problems of multinational companies for less-developed countries.

FORD OPERATIONS IN EUROPE

Ford is one of Europe's leading industrial organisations, employing some 110,000 people in 15 separate national companies. Its products are sold through 2,520 main dealers and 1460 sub-dealers across Europe. In addition there are 2,150 Ford customer service and repair centres.

1 BELFAST
2 CORK
3 HALEWOOD
4 TREFOREST
5 SWANSEA
6 BRIDGEND
7 LANGLEY
8 LEAMINGTON
9 DAVENTRY
10 SOUTHAMPTON
11 DAGENHAM/
   WARLEY/
   AVELEY
12 ENFIELD
13 WOOLWICH/
   CROYDON
14 BASILDON/
   DUNTON/
   BOREHAM
15 OSLO
16 STOCKHOLM
17 HELSINKI
18 COPENHAGEN
19 AMSTERDAM
20 ANTWERP
21 LOMMEL
22 BRUSSELS
23 WUELFRATH
24 COLOGNE
25 GENK
26 DUEREN
27 CHARLEVILLE
28 PARIS
29 SAARLOUIS
30 ZURICH
31 BORDEAUX
32 MADRID
33 LISBON
34 VALENCIA
35 VIENNA
36 SALZBURG
37 ROME
38 BERLIN

Section 10

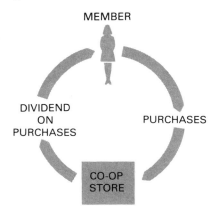

Co-operatives

In 1844 a group of poor industrial workers in Rochdale broke free of shopkeepers who sold them poor quality goods at high prices, by starting their own shop. This was the first **retail Co-operative Society**. Anyone could become a member of the Society and then share in the trading profits. A **dividend** was paid out to members according to the amount of **purchases** in the "Co-op" shop, e.g. 10p back for every £1 spent there in the year. The ideas of co-operation caught on fast — and within a century had spread all over the world.

Anyone may join a retail co-operative society for a small membership fee. A society does not rely only on these fees for the money it needs, but also has savings schemes which pay fixed interest. However, the rules state that one member has one vote, no matter how much money one may have in the society — so nobody can get to the position of dominating the society (as might a large shareholder in a company).

CHELMSFORD STAR CO-OPERATIVE SOCIETY LTD.
220, MOULSHAM STREET,
CHELMSFORD, ESSEX CM2 0LS

Registered Share Number

MEMBER'S SHARE ACCOUNT

NAME(S) IN FULL..

ADDRESS...

....

Member's Signature ....

This folder with the Current Share Account Summary must be produced whenever any money is deposited or withdrawn.

Members' meetings are held regularly, so a member can feel she has a share in how her local shops and co-op organisations are run. Funds are set aside for a variety of membership activities e.g. mens' and womens' guilds and youth clubs. Co-operative education classes are held, and the ideals of co-operative ownership are studied.

Q1 When and why was the first retail co-operative society formed?

Q2 How were the trading profits distributed to members?

Q3 How does a co-operative society get the money it needs?

Q4 How do co-operatives make sure that a society cannot be controlled by any one person?

Q5 How may members feel they have a voice in the running of their society and their local shops and Co-op affairs?

Originally there were many different town Co-op societies, each independent though linked nationally. Mergers have occurred since then, following the general pattern for larger retail organisations. Now the aim is to progress towards a single retail organisation, which would be the largest in the country. The Co-op symbol can be recognised everywhere.

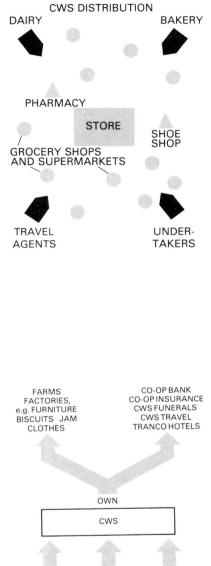

CWS DISTRIBUTION

DAIRY

BAKERY

PHARMACY

STORE

SHOE SHOP

GROCERY SHOPS AND SUPERMARKETS

TRAVEL AGENTS

UNDER-TAKERS

FARMS
FACTORIES,
e.g. FURNITURE
BISCUITS JAM
CLOTHES

CO-OP BANK
CO-OP INSURANCE
CWS FUNERALS
CWS TRAVEL
TRANCO HOTELS

OWN

CWS

OWN

CO-OP SOCIETIES

OWN

MEMBERS

In the 1960s and 1970s the return of profits to shoppers themselves was mostly made in the new form of popular trading stamps. Another change is planned for the future, when the advantage to members of shopping at the Co-op would be in the form of discounts on shop prices.

A common pattern of co-operative selling in an area is to have widespread grocery stores or supermarkets; milkrounds and bakeries; with perhaps larger central stores, e.g. Homemaker stores selling dry goods and durables (TV sets; kitchenware; DIY etc); shoe shops; pharmacies; funeral parlours or travel agencies etc.

Q6 Draw the Co-op symbol.

Q7 In what type of goods are the main sales of co-operative retail societies? Give four examples of other goods or services marketed.

In order to supply goods to retail societies, a Co-operative Wholesale Society (CWS) was formed. The CWS is owned by the retail societies, who vote in its committees according to the amount they buy from CWS. CWS buys in bulk to supply the retail societies. It has gone further, and has set up its own sources of supply — farms and factories. Their products are sold under the Co-op symbol, in competition with other manufacturers' goods in Co-op shops.

There are also CWS service organisations, e.g. the CWS bank; the Co-operative Insurance Society; travel agents; undertakers; hotels etc.

The CWS and CRS (Co-operative Retail Services) have taken over the running of retail shops in some areas during a period of mergers, development and reorganisation.

Q8 What is CWS, and what does it exist to do?

Q9 What brands are sold in Co-op shops?

Q10 Copy the diagram showing different layers of co-operative organisation and production.

Q11 List three types of goods produced by CWS; and three co-operative services.

Many new co-operative organisations have been set up over recent years — producer or worker co-operatives; housing co-operatives; agricultural co-operatives etc. All are based on the principle of common-ownership.

Other, older, and rather different societies, founded for mutual benefit or self-help rather than for profit, are Building Societies; and some Mutual Life Offices.

Q12 Think of and give a reason why worker co-operatives are springing up now.

Q13 Retail co-operative societies are one form of mutual-benefit society. Name three more.

Section 11

Public enterprise

The provision of some goods and services has been taken over by the State. Some are provided entirely out of rates and taxes, e.g. education, highways. Others are sold, e.g. electricity and rail transport, and these come under the heading of Public Enterprise.

The nation owns these **nationalised** industries. Trading profits belong to the nation. In practice profits help to finance improvements and extensions. Losses on trading are covered by the government from taxation.

Q1 What is meant by Public Enterprise?
Q2 Who owns the nationalised industries?
Q3 What happens to trading profits?
Q4 How are losses covered?

Some industries or companies were nationalised because:

a) they had to be developed nationwide and were felt too important to be left in private hands, e.g. postal services, broadcasting
b) it was felt undesirable and unnecessary to have competing companies digging up roads, e.g. for gas pipes, electric cables, water mains
c) they were essential to the nation, but private enterprise was unable to make a profit from them or to find the money neccessary for modernisation, e.g. railways and coal mines
d) the government organised the great sums necessary for development, e.g. British Airways, and oil. Profitable parts of nationalised industries may be sold off for private enterprise development.

Public enterprise may be broadly divided between
 (i) transport
 (ii) postal services
 (iii) public utilities (gas, electricity and water)
 (iv) basic industries, used by many others e.g. steel, coal, oil.

Nationalised industries may generally be recognised by the name "Board", "Authority" or "Corporation", e.g.

British Broadcasting Corporation   British Steel Corporation
Independent Broadcasting Authority   Water Authorities
British Airports Authority   National Coal Board
Electricity Boards
British Railways Board

Q5 Why have postal services come under public enterprise?
Q6 What are public utilities? Why are these services under public ownership?
Q7 Why were the railways nationalised?
Q8 What are four headings under which nationalised industries may be grouped?
Q9 Under each of these headings list the initials of a nationalised industry.

Each nationalised industry is set up by an Act of Parliament, which outlines its aims, organisation and control. The day-to-day running of each nationalised industry is in the hands of the members of a Board. The Chairman of the Board and its other members are selected by a government minister from people with experience of that industry. The Energy minister will appoint to the National Coal Board.

Once a year the Board must present its Report and Accounts to Parliament, where they are discussed. The government decides what new capital is to be provided for these industries.

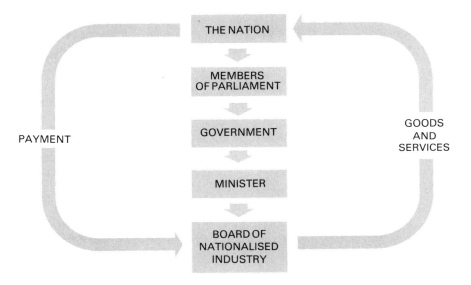

Q10 How is a nationalised industry set up?

Q11 Who is responsible for the appointment of the Board of a nationalised industry?

Q12 Who has charge of the day-to-day running of each nationalised industry?

Q13 When does Parliament review the working of a nationalised industry on behalf of the nation?

Q14 Copy the diagram showing the link between the nation and a nationalised industry.

Local authorities may also sell services e.g. tennis courts, swimming pools, transport, housing.

In some cases the act of nationalisation created a complete monopoly, (an organisation without competitors in the industry), e.g. the railways, electricity. However, electricity and gas compete with each other to supply heating and cooking, and with oil. Other nationalised bodies compete directly with private enterprise companies.

Q15 Give two examples of the sale of goods and services by local authorities.

Q16 With whom do railways compete for business?

Vocabulary

Active partner
A partner taking an active part in the running of the business.

Audited
A company's accounts examined and certified as correct by an independent firm of accountants.

Bonds
Stocks which when sold raise money for government, nationalised industries or local authorities. They pay a fixed rate of interest.

Broker-dealer
A stock**broker** operates on behalf of clients and gets a percentage commission on shares bought and sold for them. Only brokers who are members of the Stock Exchange may deal there.

Co-operative Society
A trading society owned by its members. Retail profits are distributed to members as a dividend on **purchases**.

Debenture
A loan to a public limited company over a stated period e.g. 10 years, at a fixed rate of interest.

Dividend
Share of profit distributed to shareholders (limited company); or members (co-operative societies).

Economies of scale
Savings in cost of goods produced from large-scale operation.

Equity
Ordinary shares, each of equal value.

Limited Liability
The owner only stands to lose the money invested in the business.

Limited partner
Liability ends with the capital put into the business: must be a sleeping partner.

Liquidation
The failure or bankruptcy of a limited liability company.

Market-makers
Traders in shares, specialising in certain types of companies e.g. manufacturing, oil, retailing. They buy and sell as members of the Stock Exchange.

Multinational Companies
Large companies with production units in several countries.

Ordinary shares
The main risk-bearing share, the dividend of which varies from year to year.

Partners
Several people working together for a profit, as joint owners of a business.

Proxy
Someone who is empowered to act (e.g. vote) on behalf of another.

Private enterprise
Business run to make a profit for individual owners.

Private Limited Company (Ltd)
Size: at least two shareholders. Shares may only be exchanged by private arrangement.

Public enterprise
Undertakings owned by the State or Local Authorities, selling goods or services.

Public Limited Company (PLC)
Size: at least two shareholders. Shares may be advertised to the public; and may be bought and sold freely on the Stock Exchange.

Sole trader
A business owned by one person.

Stocks
Fixed interest loans, sold on the Stock Exchange.

Stock Exchange
A market where stocks and shares are traded.

Unlimited liability
Full personal responsibility for business debts.

8 Capital and profit

All trading is a risk. The amount of profit made in a year will depend on how good the management of the business is. It may also be influenced by changes of fashion, bad weather or international crises etc.

When people are risking their money in a business in the hope of making a good profit, very careful accounts must be kept. They will want to know what the expenses of the business are, and to calculate how much clear profit has been made, compared with the amount of money (or capital) put into the business.

Sections
1. Capital
2. Mark-up   Turnover rate   Trading account
3. Profit and loss account
4. Businesses' need for money
5. Return on capital   Profit on turnover

Section 1

Capital

The aim of private enterprise business is to make a profit. The amount of profit made in a year will depend on how successful is the enterprise and management of the business. However, profit is also affected by influences outside the firm, by changes in fashion; by international crises; or even by the weather. All trading is a risk. When people are risking their money in a business in the hope of making a good profit, very careful accounts must be kept. They will want to know the total takings for the year; what the expenses of the business are; and how much clear profit has been made in a period.

Capital is the name given to the money first put in by the owner(s) to run a business. A **balance sheet** accounts for what has been done with that money, on two equal or balancing sides, and shows the state of the business at a particular date. If, on 5 May A Trader puts £10,000 into a business bank account in order to start trading, a balance sheet of the business on that day would show all its **assets** (what it owns) in the bank.

Balance Sheet
of A Trader at 5 April 1987

	£	Assets	£
Capital	10,000	Bank	10,000
	10,000		10,000

Assets

First, he will want to buy the necessary equipment to run the business — furniture and fittings, machinery, vans etc. These items of **capital equipment** are **fixed capital**, not for resale, but to be used again and again in running the business. On a balance sheet capital equipment items are listed as **fixed assets**.

Circulating capital is the name given to the money and stocks used in day-to-day trade to make a profit. Stocks of goods will be sold at a profit, and replaced, for further sales. Circulating capital changes its form, circulating from money into stocks, and through sales back to money again. These items are listed on a balance sheet as **current assets**.

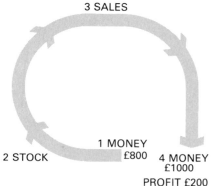

3 SALES

2 STOCK

1 MONEY
£800   4 MONEY
£1000
PROFIT £200

Q1 a) Copy the diagram of circulating capital.
b) Goods are bought at cost price and sold at selling price. What is the difference in value between the two?

Q2 Imagine you are starting your own hairdressing salon. Name four items you might buy as fixed assets.

Q3 List four items that a hairdressing salon might stock for use in the course of everyday business, and replace, as part of current assets.

Q4 List four fixed assets you might find as part of a) a clothing manufacturing business; and b) a grocery business.

Q5 Where does the capital to start a business come from with a) a sole trader; b) partners; c) a limited liability company?

Balance Sheet
of A Trader at 5 May 1987

	£	Assets	£
Capital	10,000	Fixed Assets	
		Equipment	1,000
		Vehicle	5,000
		Current Assets	
		Stock	500
		Bank	3,500
	10,000		10,000

Liabilities

The capital **owned** in a business is not the only money **used** in that business. Premises may be bought on a mortgage: they belong to the business, but at the same time money is owed, and the business is responsible or **liable** for repayment. Stock is normally bought from suppliers on credit, and money owed to them is totalled under the heading **creditors**. On a balance sheet all money used in a business is listed under the heading **liabilities** and balances its assets. Liabilities include trade creditors (suppliers of stock); mortgages; and loans (e.g. from a bank) as well as capital (considered as repayable to the owners).

Profit

By the end of each year a new position will have been reached, and a new balance sheet is drawn up. Stock will have been sold (and replaced) and a profit made. Takings will have been paid into the bank. If stock sold has not yet been paid for by customers, debts are owed to the business, and are listed under **debtors** on the assets side of the balance sheet. When the debts are paid, the money will swell the bank.

Any profits will belong to the owners of the business. If the profits are left in the business, the increase in assets, from bank or debtors, would be matched by increasing the capital on the liabilities side of a balance sheet.

Some of the annual profit will be distributed to the owners, however (e.g. as dividends or drawings), and withdrawn from the business. Part of the profit is generally left in, or "ploughed back" into the business to increase its capital and to help finance future expansion.

Q6 What is shown by a balance sheet?

Q7 What are the two sides of a balance sheet called?

Q8 What items are listed under current assets? What is meant by debtors?

Q9 What name is given to the suppliers to the firm of stock on credit?

Q10 Study the two balance sheets as at 5 May 1987 and 5 May 1988. At each date, what was a) the capital owned; b) the capital used in the business; c) the total fixed assets; and d) the total current assets.

Q11 Draw up a balance sheet in the same form from the following information: premises £76,000; furniture and fixtures £5,000; equipment £4,000; vehicle £5,000; stock £6,000; debtors £400; bank £3,600; capital £65,000; mortgage £30,000; bank loan £4,000; creditors £1,000.

Balance Sheet of A Trader at 5 May 1988

Liabilities		£	Assets	£
Capital	10,000		**Fixed Assets**	
+ Profit	2,000		Equipment	3,000
			Furniture & Fittings	2,000
− Drawings	1,000		Vehicle	5,000
		11,000	**Current Assets**	
			Stock	1,000
Loan (Bank)	5,000		Debtors	200
Trade Creditors		400	Bank	5,200
		16,400		16,400

Section 2

Mark-up

In order to make a profit, a retail business buys goods (e.g. from a wholesaler) and resells them (to the consumer) at a higher price.

Mark-up is the amount added to the cost price of each item to reach its selling price. Mark-up is generally given as a percentage of the cost price.

Example

Cost Price + Mark-up = Selling Price	Mark-up as percentage of Cost Price
£100 + £50 = £150	$\frac{50}{100} \times 100 = 50\%$
£10 + £10 = £20	$\frac{10}{10} \times 100 = 100\%$

Q1 a) If the cost of an article was £5, and the mark-up is £2.50, what is the selling price?

b) If the selling price of an article is £15, and the mark-up is £5, what was its cost price?

c) If goods are sold at £100, marked-up from £75 cost, what mark-up was allowed?

d) Copy the table below and complete the blanks.

Cost Price	Mark-Up	Selling Price
£15	. . . .	£17.50
. . . .	£8	£18
£110	£50	. . . .

Q2 Copy and complete the table below, calculating mark-up as a percentage of the cost price in each case.

CP	MU	SP	MU as % of CP
£100	. . . .	£120	$\frac{. . .}{. . .} \times 100 = ...$
. . . .	£5	£15	. . . .
£20	. . . .	£30	. . . .
£7.50	£7.50	. . . .	. . . .

Turnover rate

To make a trading profit of £1,000, a trader might sell 1000 goods at £1 profit on each, or 200 goods at £5 profit on each. The rate of mark-up varies from one type of trade to another. If goods are sold fast, every day, the mark-up can be low, e.g. on groceries. If goods move slowly, e.g. antiques, a higher mark-up will be needed. **Turnover** is the name given to the total value of sales during a period, e.g. one year. The **rate of turnover** or **stock turn** shows how fast goods are sold and replaced, or "turned over" on the shelves.

To find stock turn, a trader will calculate how often stock is replaced in a year, by dividing his average-stock-held into the value of stock sold. To calculate average stock, the stock at the beginning and at the end of the year, e.g. January and December $\div 2$ is used: this avoids too-frequent stocktaking, e.g.:

Stock held at 1 Jan 1985 = £300
Stock held at 31 Dec 1985 = £700

$$\text{Average stock} = \frac{300 + 700}{2} = £500$$

Stock Turn

$$\frac{\text{Cost of stock sold}}{\text{Cost of average stock}} \qquad \frac{5,000}{500} = \quad 10$$

The stock he holds is recorded at its cost price, so in order to make a fair comparison, it is the cost price of the goods sold that must be taken, not the selling price.

Q3 a) If the mark-up on an article is £5, how much has been made on the sale of 10 articles?
  b) If CP = £20 and SP = £30, what profit is made on the sale of 12 items?
  c) If SP = £100 on an item which cost the trader £70, what profit does he make on the sale of 5 items?

Q4 Why is the mark-up higher on antiques than on groceries?

Q5 Give three examples of businesses with a) a fast turnover; and b) a slow turnover of goods.

Q6 If a trader found on stocktaking that he had £2,000 stock in January, and £4,000 in December of a year, what would be his average stock?

Q7 If the average stock held by a shop cost £1,000, and the cost of the goods sold in the year was £50,000, what was the rate of stock turn?

Q8 If the average stock held by a business cost £200 and the monthly rate of stock turn was 10, what would be the expected monthly turnover, at cost price?

Trading account

A **Trading Account** shows a business how much trading profit it has made in a year. On one side of the account is set out the total received for the goods sold in the year, and on the other side the cost of those goods. The difference is the trading profit, or **Gross Profit**: this gives balancing totals on the two sides of the account.

Q9 If a trader buys stock at £6,000 and sells it all for £7,500, find his gross profit by setting out a Trading Account.

Q10 A trader sold goods for £10,000 at a profit of £3,000. Set out a Trading Account (calculating the cost price of goods sold).

Trading Account
for the year ended 5 May 1988

	£		£
Cost price of goods sold	6,000	Sales	9,000
Gross profit	3,000		
	9,000		9,000

Section 3

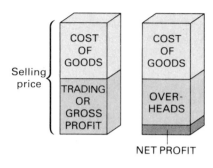

Profit and loss account

The Gross Profit made from trading in a year is shown in a Trading Account. However, in addition to the cost of stock, there are many other expenses that have to be taken into account. For all businesses there are also the costs of selling the goods, and of running the business, the **administrative costs**. Some expenses are directly related to sales, such as sales commission, or delivery. The overall expenses to be met are rent, rates, cleaning, telephone, etc. They are always hanging over the head of the business and must be paid whether or not a good profit has been made. These are called **overheads**. Only after overheads and sales expenses have been met can a trader know his true or **Net Profit**.

Bills may come in at different times, monthly, quarterly or yearly. All the information is brought together annually, in the **Profit and Loss Account**, to see exactly what success the business has had. The year's Gross Profit (the firm's income or **revenue**) is brought down from the Trading Account on one side: and against this are set out the expenses that must be met out of it, the **revenue expenses**. The difference remaining, to balance the two sides, is the Net Profit.

Q1 Describe in your own words what is meant by Net Profit.

Q2 Why is the overall profit position of a firm only known periodically, e.g. once a year?

Q3 Make two lists headed **capital spending** and **revenue spending**, from the following items of expenditure.

rent	insurance	heat and light
machinery	repairs to old van	salaries
telephone	new van	
advertising	new typewriter	

Q4 If a firm's Gross Profit is £20,000, and all its overheads and selling expenses add up to £15,000, what is its Net Profit?

Q5 Explain the difference between Gross and Net Profit.

Q6 What is meant by overheads? Give five examples.

Q7 Draw up a Profit and Loss Account from the following items, and find the Net Profit.
Gross Profit £10,000; rates £500; insurance £200; heat and light £300; telephone £200; salaries £5,000; advertising £500; cleaning £300.

Profit and Loss Account
for the year ended 5 May 1988

	£		£
Rent	500	Gross	
Electricity	200	profit	3,000
Cleaning	100		
Stationery	100		
Advertising	100		
Net profit	2,000		
	3,000		3,000

If expenses were larger than the Gross Profit, then a Net Loss would be made. Over many years a company will gain experience of how much its total expenses are likely to be in relation to its total sales or turnover. This will affect the percentage mark-up on the cost price of the goods. The mark-up must be high enough to cover all expenses for the business to **break even**. An expense that must be taken into account, for example, is the wear-and-tear on capital equipment, e.g. using up the "life" of vehicles or machinery. The allowance made for this is called **depreciation**. Mark-up must not only cover expenses but allow for profit as well.

Q8 One year, the cost of goods sold was £6,000, and the expenses on the Profit and Loss Account were £3,000. What would have to be:
a) the total of sales or turnover to break even; and
b) the percentage of mark-up on cost?

Q9 What is meant by depreciation?

Q10 If the cost of a vehicle is £5,000 and it is expected to last 10 years before replacement, how much would be allowed for depreciation a year, or using-up-of-the-asset?

Case Study
Joan Reed decides to use her redundancy money to buy a street corner shop to sell newspapers, magazines, sweets and other small items, pens, etc. Nearby are a school and a factory; and the streets become crowded at lunchtime. She decides to lease a heating cabinet and rotisserie to sell roast chicken pieces and hot snacks; and to hire purchase a freezing cabinet to sell ice creams.

Q12 Read the Case Study above. If Joan takes £250 a week on hot snacks:
a) What will be her monthly (four-week) turnover?
b) If the uncooked stocks cost £400 per month, what would be her Gross Profit for the year on hot snacks?
c) If the lease of the equipment cost £4,000 a year, what would be her Net Profit on this line?

Q13 Hire purchase payments on the cold cabinet were £150 a month. In the three hottest months, she made £400 a month on top of the cost of stocks. In each of the three coldest months she made £150 a month. In spring and autumn she made £250 a month. What would be her annual net profit:
a) while she was paying off the HP?
b) when she had completed HP payments?

Q14 Set out the advantages to Joan Reed of the lease or hire purchase of the equipment, instead of outright purchase.

Section 4

Businesses need money

Most businesses are in want of more money.

1. If they are doing well they want more money to expand.
2. If they are doing badly, they want help to keep going, and pay their suppliers.
3. Machinery may need replacing, without the firm having the necessary capital to purchase new machinery.
4. A business may consider moving to a cheaper area. This would bring long-term advantages, but result in short-term disruption and expense.
5. A firm may be confident of good profits at a certain season e.g. Christmas; but it needs a loan to buy-in the necessary extra stocks.
6. Sometimes a firm has recorded a good trading profit in its accounts, the **books**; but the debtors are slow to pay what they owe. In the meantime, it may have difficulty in finding cash to pay its own suppliers, in its **cash flow**.
7. A company may have to work for months with heavy expenses or outgoings, before it gets fully paid on completion of the job, as with building works. Here again the problem is not making a sale, but carrying on until payment is completed.
8. It may be the custom to allow a six-month period of credit on sales, in, say, the export trade. The firm may need a loan or **advance** against debtors (money owing on sales).

Borrowing from a bank

A business in need of money is likely to turn first to a bank. It needs to satisfy the bank that extra profit is likely to result from a loan, enough to benefit the firm and pay back the loan with interest, in an agreed time. A bank wants to make a profit (interest), but is always cautious, because it is responsible for other people's money which it is using. The bank will study and compare the firm's Trading and Profit and Loss Accounts and Balance Sheets over several years, together with careful forecasts of sales and expenses in a period, i.e. cash flow, in and out.

Q1 What is the main consideration of the bank when deciding whether to agree a loan?

Q2 Study the eight examples given above of business' need for money. Select four examples where a bank is most likely to grant a loan or overdraft, because least risk is involved, i.e. since sales have already been made or can be expected from past experience. Explain your choice.

Q3 Select two further cases in which sales levels in the future are more uncertain. For what figures would the bank ask the firm in each case, before making a decision, and why?

Q4 In which case would the bank manager be likely to refuse a loan, and why?

Case Study

Peter Jackson was made redundant from an engineering company and was unable to find another job in the same line of business. He decided to earn money becoming a driver for a car hire firm. After a few months he determined to start his own car hire business, with his wife's help, to reap the full profit of the trade.

He had some cards printed, and distributed these door-to-door round a wide area. He found that he was living on his savings for the first few months, but after that his business picked up, as he built up his contacts. A year later he was making more money than he ever did working for the engineering company. Sometimes he even had to turn away business because he was so busy. He was convinced he could do even better with more cars, and he saved carefully to have some capital available to plough back into the business. He looked forward to having an office in the High Street, a small fleet of radio-cars, and a maintenance garage.

He arranged an interview with his bank manager to discuss a loan, taking his estimates with him.

Q5 Give four sets of figures that the bank manager might require from Peter Jackson.

Q6 The bank manager would want to know how much of his own capital Jackson was risking. Why do you think the bank considers this important?

Q7 Even without a bank loan, would Jackson have to find the full purchase price for a) premises, b) vehicles? What other alternatives are open to him?

Q8 Why might a bank manager be more ready to agree a loan for seasonal stock rather than for long-term fixed capital (e.g. new premises or equipment)?

Q9 Does the owner of a business reckon to pocket the whole profit made in a year? Explain your answer.

Q10 Why might the owners of a business prefer to finance a planned expansion themselves, as much as possible, rather than seek a bank loan or HP agreements?

Section 5

Return on capital

Profit is uncertain for many reasons, e.g. fashion changes; international crises; the quality of management. That is why money invested in business is called Risk Capital. The higher the risk, the larger **return** on capital will be looked for, i.e. in profit or interest.

The return is judged by finding the percentage of profits to capital. This enables one investment to be compared with another.

Example

A profit of £10,000 is good on a capital of £20,000 (50%) but disappointing on a capital of £200,000 (5%).

Q1 Give two examples of business risks which affect the sale of
a) ice cream b) holidays in Turkey.

Q2 Why do many boutiques go out of business?

Q3 If a profit of £200 has been made by two businesses, one employing a capital of £2,000 and the other £4,000, which business has made the higher return on capital?

Q4 If two people start in business with a capital of £5,000 each, and at the end of the year one has made a return on capital of 100 per cent and the other 50 per cent, what is the difference in the actual sums earned?

Q5 If you can get 9 per cent interest on a Savings Bank account, do you think it is worth putting money into a business for the same estimated return? Give reasons for your answer.

Q6 If Business A employs £40,000 capital and makes £10,000 profit, is it using its resources better or worse than Business B which employs £100,000 capital and makes £20,000 profit?

Q7 A small business employs £2,500 capital, and in a year has made £900 profit. A larger business employs £50,000 capital, and in the same year made £16,000 profit. Which business had the better return on capital?

The owners' capital may not be the only funds used in a business. A long-term loan also counts as **capital employed** or used in making a profit.

Case Study

Jason Stock starts a business with £50,000 and makes a profit of £10,000 in the first year. The next year he expands, with a further £28,000 brought into the business by a new partner, Errol Brown, and a loan of £6,000 from Jason's father. The second year's profit is £21,000.

Year 1:
Profit of £10,000 on capital employed of £50,000 is 20%.

Year 2:
Profit of £21,000 on capital employed of £84,000
(£50,000 + £28,000 + £6,000) is 25%.

There was a higher return on capital employed in the second year.

The partners agreed to divide profits in the ratio 2:1. Jason was to get twice as much as Errol as he had started the business and brought in nearly twice as much capital
In Year 1 Jason got all the profit = £10,000.
In Year 2 he got $\frac{2}{3}$ of the profit = £14,000, so he had not lost by taking a partner.
Errol's return was £7,000 on his capital of £28,000. This was much higher than he could have got on interest from savings: so he was well pleased.

Q8 In the Case Study above, what was Jason Stock's return on his capital in year 2?
Q9 What was Errol's return on his capital?
Q10 One year a trader made a profit of 200 per cent on capital of £1,000. The trader was determined to expand, and borrowed another £1,000 from the bank. The next year the profit was £3,000. Had a higher return been earned on capital employed?
Q11 Margaret Addison puts £8,000 into a business, and makes a profit of £2,000 in the first year. She borrows £7,000, and makes £3,000 profit in year 2, and £5,000 in year 3. What was her return on capital employed in each year?

Profit on turnover

To compare one year's success with another, profit may be judged as a percentage of **turnover** or total sales. The **gross** profit figure will show trading profits only. The **net** profit figure will take into account costs of selling, and overhead and administrative expenses.

Example
Net profit of £10,000 on sales of £50,000 is 20%.

Net profit of £10,000 on turnover of £40,000 is 25%.

Q12 Business A made a gross profit of £24,000 on a turnover of £80,000. Business B made a gross profit of £8,000 on a turnover of £24,000. Compare the gross profit on sales of the two businesses.
Q13 If Business A above had total expenses of £4,000; and Business B's total expenses were £2,000, which business achieved the highest percentage of net profit to turnover?
Q14 The ABC Co. had a turnover of £100,000 and made a gross profit of £45,000. Their percentage of net profit to turnover was 20 per cent. The XYZ Co. had a turnover of £50,000 and made a gross profit of £20,000. Their percentage of net profit to turnover was 24 per cent. For each business find the percentage of gross profit to turnover; and compare the running of the two businesses from all the figures.

Vocabulary

Administrative costs
The costs of managing a business, e.g. office costs.

Advance
A loan advanced against debts, i.e. sales made but not yet paid for by customers.

Assets
Everything owned by a business.

Balance Sheet
An account of the money used by a business, and what has been done with that money.

Books
The accounts of a business.

Break even
The point at which takings cover all expenses.

Budget
Plan for expenditure against expected income.

Capital
Money, or money's-worth, used to run a business.

Capital equipment
(see Fixed assets)

Cash flow
The money flowing into or out of a business, e.g. takings and expenses.

Circulating capital or current assets
The cycle of money used to buy stocks which, after sales, returns to money again.

Creditors
People owed money, e.g. for goods supplied on credit.

Debtors
People owing debts to the business, e.g. for goods bought.

Depreciation
Allowance made for using up the "life" of capital equipment in a year.

Fixed assets or capital
Premises, equipment, vehicles etc. kept for use in the running of a business.

Gross Profit
Profit made from trading i.e. the difference between cost price and selling price.

Liabilities
Money for which a business is responsible. Money owing, e.g. for loans and to trade creditors.

Mark-up
The amount or percentage added to the cost of an article to arrive at the selling price.

Net Profit
The final or clear profit made, after all expenses have been paid out of gross profit.

Overheads
Fixed expenses of a business e.g. rent, rates, electricity.

Profit and Loss Account
Account setting out the expenses to be paid out of trading (gross) profit, to arrive at the final or Net Profit.

Retained profit
Profit kept in the business instead of being withdrawn for the owners.

Return on capital
The money earned from investment.

Revenue expenses
Running expenses that are met out of revenue or takings.

Risk capital
Money invested in business, where the size of profit is always uncertain.

Stock turn
The rate at which stock is sold, and replaced.

Trading Account
The account setting out the cost of stocks, the value of sales, and the Gross Profit made on trading.

Turnover
The total value of sales during a period e.g. one year.

9 Transport

Transport is a commercial service essential to trade. Raw materials are transported to the factory, often between one country and another. Goods are distributed from factory to warehouse and from warehouse to retailer, e.g. by rail or road. Transport costs affect the price of goods in the shops; and transport is highly competitive, not only between transport firms, and between public and private enterprise, but between road and rail, air and sea transport. Choice is made as to the method of transport by considering cost, convenience, safety and speed.

Section
1. Passenger Transport (1)   By Road   By Rail
2. Passenger Transport (2)   British Rail   By Air
3. Passenger Transport (3)   By Water   Scheduled Lines and Chartered Transport
4. The Container Revolution   Forwarding or Shipping Agents
5. Goods Transport (1)   By Rail
6. Goods Transport (2)   By Road   National Freight Co. Ltd
7. Goods Transport (3)   By Water   Canals   Coastal Shipping   Ocean Shipping
8. The Baltic Exchange   Bill of Lading
9. Goods Transport (4)   By Air

Section 1

Passenger Transport (1)

We have a choice as to how to travel — by road or rail, by air or water. Our choice will depend on the **distance**, the **cost**, the **convenience** and the **speed**. It has been said that improvements in transport have made the world smaller. This seems so because it is now much quicker and easier for people to travel long distances for business and pleasure.

By road

Convenience is a major advantage of travelling by car, either privately owned or hired. You are taken from door to door; you can start when you wish; and stop wherever you please. Britain has a fine network of main and secondary roads.

The cost of travelling by car is generally thought of as the price of the petrol used. The full cost is seldom added up of repairs and replacement, insurance and tax for the individual vehicle, let alone the cost of the road system, traffic control, accidents etc.

The cost of going away on holiday for a family of four is cheapest in their own car. However, the journey for a driver alone becomes much more expensive.

Coach transport is cheaper than rail, though slower over a long distance. Coaches are very convenient for outings, and economical if there is a full coach load.

Q1 What is meant by saying that improvements in transport have "made the world smaller"?

Q2 What are the main considerations when choosing between different types of transport?

Q3 List five private means of transport owned by individuals.

Q4 What are four advantages of travelling in your own car?

Q5 List one advantage and one disadvantage of long-distance travel by coach.

The number of private cars on the road is rising by 10 per cent each year. The popularity of driving is creating its own problems, e.g. traffic jams, parking difficulties and petrol consumption.

Fewer people now use buses and bus services have been cut — making a poorer passenger service for those not in cars. It is a problem for buses whether to attract passengers with low fares and frequent services, or whether to meet rising costs by raising fares and cutting services. Most bus services are run by public enterprise, e.g. London Regional Transport (Board) or NBC (National Bus Company). Private enterprise also takes a hand in passenger transport.

Q6 Give four problems linked with private car ownership.

Q7 Give two present problems for bus services.

Q8 Name two nationalised bodies running bus services.

By Rail

The advantage of rail transport is **speed** over long distances, without traffic hold-ups. Passengers can move around in corridor trains and there are toilets. Sleepers, buffet and restaurant cars may be provided. The disadvantage of rail transport is having to get to and from the station, and of having to catch a train at a fixed time.

Thousands of commuters travelling daily to work in big cities rely on trains, and rush-hour services are very crowded. Inter-city expresses link large towns.

British Rail offer many schemes to attract passengers: Inter-City Weekend reductions; AwayDay Off-Peak tickets; party reductions; Rover tickets; weekend hotel offers and holiday packages; Motorail; and Rail-Drive arrangements with car-hire.

Q9 List the advantages of rail for long distance journeys.

Q10 Give seven ways in which British Rail tries to attract passengers.

Section 2

Passenger Transport

British Rail

Railways were developed in the middle of the last century, whereas motor cars only came into common use after the end of the First World War in 1918. The costs of running a railway are very high, e.g. rails, rolling stock (engines, carriages and waggons), stations, bridges, tunnels, signals, and the labour needed to maintain and run the network. In every country the railways run at a loss. In Europe all railways have been nationalised so that the State makes up the loss. Railways are too important to be neglected.

British Rail is responsible for all railways services in the United Kingdom. They also link with ferry services covering the short sea crossings, e.g. to Europe, Ireland, the Isle of Wight and with the rail services beyond.

The ferry services run by Sealink, the largest of the cross-channel companies.

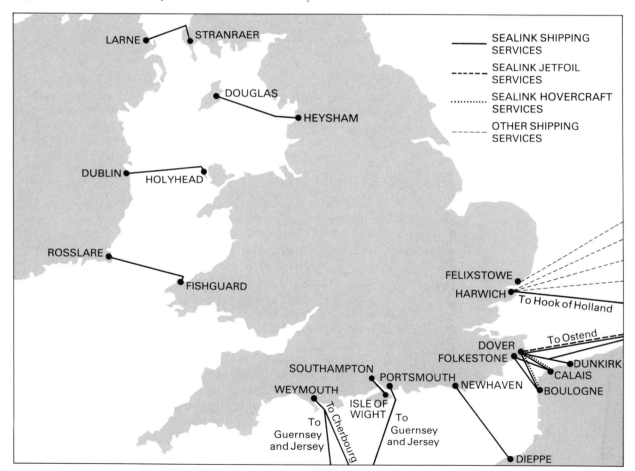

Q1 List five costs of running a railway.

Q2 List five ferry services, naming the ports at each end.

Q3 Discuss the advantages and disadvantages of road and rail transport for:
- a) a party of 35 pensioners on a day's outing to the seaside 70 kilometres away
- b) 30 school children visiting a town hall two kilometres away
- c) a grandmother travelling 200 kilometres to see her son
- d) a family with a baby and a toddler going on holiday 120 kilometres away.

By Air

Air transport has the advantage of **speed**, but is generally more expensive than other forms of travel. For a highly-paid businessman it is important to waste as little time as possible in travelling. The growth of trade-links and the growing popularity of holidays abroad have boosted air travel between countries.

Internal air travel has also been growing fast, even in Britain where distances are comparatively short, and where the time of a flight may be doubled by the drive to and from the airfield and weighing-in at the airport. Large companies may own a light cabin aircraft to transport top managers round the country.

In a country of vast distances or mountain ranges, planes may be the most common form of transport across country, e.g. in Australia, USSR, South America.

Nearly every country runs a national airline, and there are also lines run in competition by privately-owned companies. The main British airline, **British Airways**, has divisions covering Europe, and the rest of the world.

Q4 Why has air travel increased so much in recent years?

Q5 What is the main advantage of air travel and what are the disadvantages?

Q6 In some countries air travel is more common than long distance road or rail transport. Give two examples and explain the reasons why.

Q7 Has Britain internal flights? What are the drawbacks?

Q8 From what countries are the following airlines?
- a) Lufthansa
- b) Quantas
- c) El Al
- d) Pan-Am
- e) Sabina
- f) Trans-World Airlines (TWA)

Q9 Name two privately owned UK airlines.

Section 3

Passenger Transport (3)

By Water

Less fuel is needed to pull a load that floats through water, than along the ground or into the air. Water transport is therefore generally **cheaper** than other methods, but is also slower.

Britain has an indented coastline with many good harbours. Different ports have been developed for links with different countries, e.g. Liverpool facing westwards to America; east coast ports for the Continent; south coast ports for France, Spain, the Mediterranean and Africa.

Ocean liners, e.g. on the Atlantic crossing, are luxurious and offer healthy relaxation with swimming pools, deck games, dances, cinemas and much entertainment and elaborate menus. For the business person secretarial services and radio-telephone are available.

The Channel is a very busy seaway. Ferries cross from Britain to the Continent several times a day from a number of ports in southern England. Passenger ferries and hovercraft run from Harwich, Ramsgate, Dover, Folkstone, Southampton and Weymouth to Holland, Belgium and France.

Holiday cruises are popular, with ships like floating hotels, visiting ports of interest. Peaceful barge holidays on British canals are growing in popularity, and our coasts, rivers and lakes are used for pleasure sailing.

To the Baltic and North Europe

To America

•LIVERPOOL

•HULL

FELIXSTOWE •

LONDON •

DOVER •

To EEC

SOUTHAMPTON•

To Mediterranean and Far East

Q1 What is the main advantage of water transport and the main disadvantage?

Q2 Name six ports in Britain. What areas might be served by shipping lines from a) Liverpool b) Southampton?

Q3 Give reasons why people might choose to cross the Atlantic by sea instead of by air.

Q4 Describe three ways in which Britain's waterways are used for leisure activities.

Scheduled lines and chartered transport

A transport line runs to a regular schedule with fixed stops, i.e airlines, railways lines, shipping lines, and bus and coach services. The line is expected to run however many passengers are on board. The price charged has to cover the cost of empty seats on some journeys.

On the other hand, hired or chartered transport works out much cheaper per person if all the seats are filled. Coaches are frequently hired for a Works' or Club outing. Tour operators can offer bargains on package holidays using charter planes.

Q5 What is meant by a scheduled line?

Q6 Give two examples where transport may be chartered.

Q7 Why may chartered transport work out much cheaper than scheduled transport, per person?

Q8 Think of and discuss three reasons why a hired coach may be chosen for an outing.

Q9 Travel agents organise different mixes of the four main types of transport to obtain advantages of speed and cost. Think of three different transport packages between London and Paris, giving the advantages of each.

Q10 What transport do you think would be chosen by a pop group on a country-wide tour and why?

Section 4

The Container Revolution

Transport is used for all goods between factory and shop. It is aimed to make transport ever quicker, cheaper, safer and easier. **Containers** can both provide protection for goods and be easily handled mechanically between one carrier and another with a great saving of time. The improvement in the speed and ease of handling goods or "freight" has been called "the Container Revolution".

Containers can be easily hauled on trailers. They are locked into position and there is far less danger of damage or pilferage (petty theft) so insurance rates are lower.

At **Container Terminals** containers are transferred between road and rail transport by gantry crane in two minutes. A whole train load of containers can be cleared in an hour on to lorries for delivery and vice versa.

Containers are weatherproof and can be stacked in the open. They are made in standard sizes and can be easily moved and stacked.

Containers may be shipped as deck cargo. Special container ships are designed to hold three storeys of containers below decks and two above. These ships can be unloaded and reloaded within 24 hours, 10 times quicker than ordinary general cargo ships.

Container Ports have been specially built for container traffic. These provide large container parking sites behind deep shipping-berths, with easy access for road and rail. Special long-armed cranes load and unload the container ships.

Q1 How is it aimed to improve the transport of freight?

Q2 Why is insurance cheaper for containerised goods?

Q3 What is a container terminal?

Q4 How do containers save on warehousing costs?

Q5 Describe a specially-designed container ship.

Q6 What is meant by "the Container Revolution"?

Q7 What are the special features of a container port?

Forwarding or Shipping Agents

Forwarding or Shipping Agents are specialist companies that plan the best transport for goods, and will see to all the necessary arrangements and documents (forms, insurance etc). They may act as agents for the seller (the consignor) or the buyer (the consignee).

A Consignment Note is given by a transport organisation, e.g. British Rail, as a receipt for the goods, to the consignor.

Q8 What is a Forwarding Agent?

Q9 What is a Consignment Note?

Section 5

Goods transport (1)

By rail

Britain has a fine railway network and this is run as a nationalised enterprise by British Rail. It is extremely difficult to run a railway system at a profit owing to the heavy running costs; but the railways are so important to the country that losses are covered by taxation. In the interests of economy, rail traffic has been concentrated on to main lines, which have been electrified and modernised; many lesser-used branch lines have been closed.

Railways cannot carry goods door-to-door, and for journeys under 200 miles, with transfer of goods from-lorry-to-train-to-lorry again, is not worthwhile. For journeys of over 200 miles, however, goods can travel faster by rail — without traffic jams. Rail is particularly good for long-distance heavy loads. The main freight carried by British Rail is coal, iron and steel, petrol, cars, cement and building materials.

There are many types of railway waggon to suit different types of load and usage. British Rail negotiate special contracts with some companies for the bulk transport of goods, e.g. with a Mail Order House. British Rail lorries will collect and deliver goods from the station.

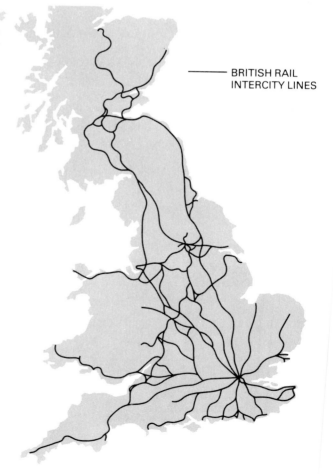

——— BRITISH RAIL INTERCITY LINES

A company may hire waggons from British Rail. Companies may have private sidings, and a "company train" is timetabled by British Rail on to main lines at off-peak times, to travel between the company's depots (stores) or factories.

Freightliners are all-container freight expresses. The containers will be delivered anywhere in the country within 24 hours.

Merry-Go-Round trains follow a circular route round the country for the collection and delivery of coal, iron and steel at many sites. Coal hopper waggons can be top-loaded and bottom-emptied while the train crawls forward.

Roll-On-Roll-Off ferries carry vehicles and passengers. Some are fitted with rails to carry railway waggons and carriages on to Continental lines. Lines have the same gauge or width up to the borders of Spain and the USSR.

Q1 Who owns the railways in Britain?

Q2 a) Why is it difficult to run a railway at a profit?
b) Who covers losses?

Q3 What measures have been taken to reduce railway losses?

Q4 For what type of journey and load is rail transport best suited?

Q5 What are the main types of goods carried by rail?

Q6 List three types of railway waggon, and the goods that may be carried in them.

Q7 What is a Freightliner?

Q8 Describe the special arrangements for the transport of coal.

Q9 What is a company train?

Q10 What is a roll-on, roll-off ferry?

Section 6

Goods transport (2)

By road

Road goods traffic can be divided between a) local, for deliveries etc; b) long-distance haulage. Transport firms carry loads for customers. However, many large companies have their own fleets of lorries and vans displaying their names.

Motorways are constructed to speed long-distance traffic, by-passing towns. The planning of the road system comes under the Department of Transport. Over two-thirds of all goods-transport is now by road. The main advantages are the convenience of being able to load up at the factory door in their own time; goods being undisturbed door-to-door; and the saving of cost, if a full load is arranged going out and coming back.

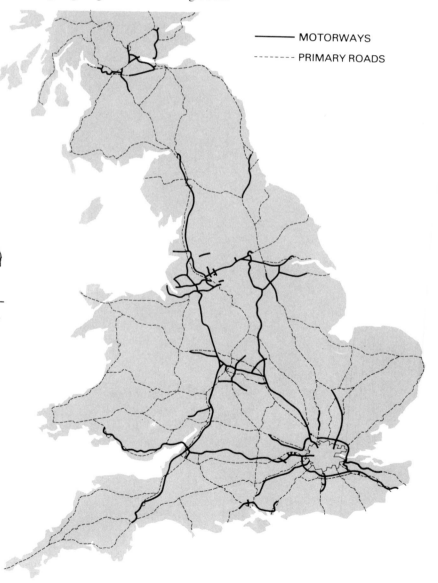

— MOTORWAYS
------- PRIMARY ROADS

In addition to driving licences, vehicle owners pay road tax. Special licences are required for a) heavy vehicles; and b) passenger carrying. More is collected in tax from road users than is spent on motorways. However, there are many social costs borne by the community, for example traffic control, accidents, pollution and noise. The size and weight of trailer loads have increased in recent years, so that one driver carries more goods. There has been a public outcry against the steady increase in heavy traffic and the damage to road surfaces and to villages from juggernauts.

Goods are exported from Britain to Europe by lorry, using roll-on roll-off ferries. The TIR sign (Transport Internationale Routier) shows that a container has been sealed by Customs at the start of the journey and need not be opened and examined at every frontier.

Q1 What are the two types of road transport of goods?

Q2 What money does the State collect from vehicle owners?

Q3 Give three types of licence for driving vehicles.

Q4 List three advantages of road freight transport.

Q5 Why is road transport used for most freight? Discuss whether it is always cheaper than rail.

Q6 List three hidden social costs of road transport.

Q7 How can goods be exported from Britain "by road"?

Q8 Explain the meaning of TIR.

The **National Freight Corporation** was a nationalised body, set up to co-ordinate goods transport between road and rail. Nationally it was thought to make sense to use rail (Freightliners) for distances over 200 miles, and to have a system of local delivery by road in a radius round the large rail depots. However, in 1982 the NFC was denationalised. Its employees decided to continue to run it as private enterprise. The National Freight Consortium PLC is now almost entirely owned by present and past employees and their families. It controls a variety of road transport services, including British Road Services Ltd; Pickfords Removals Ltd; National Carriers Ltd; and Roadline UK Ltd for parcels deliveries.

Q9 Who owns the National Freight Consortium PLC?

Q10 List the names of four road service companies run by the National Freight Consortium.

Section 7

Goods transport (3)

By water

On water, heavy loads can be floated, and then moved with less fuel than would be needed for transport on land or air. Water transport is therefore cheaper than other forms, but it is slower. It is particularly suitable for bulk loads not urgently required.

There are three types of water transport:
  inland — by canal
  coastal — round the coast
  ocean — long distance.

Canals

A network of canals was dug in England in the eighteenth century before railways were developed, to carry coal etc. Canal traffic is slowed by the number of locks necessary to convey boats from one water level to another across country. Canals link the four large English estuaries with the industrial Midlands. The main goods carried are: coal, petrol, stone and clay, building materials and timber.

Canals are under the control of the British Waterways Board, who charge certain fees to users. They also hire out barges, in competition with private barge owners. Canals are being increasingly used for pleasure boating.

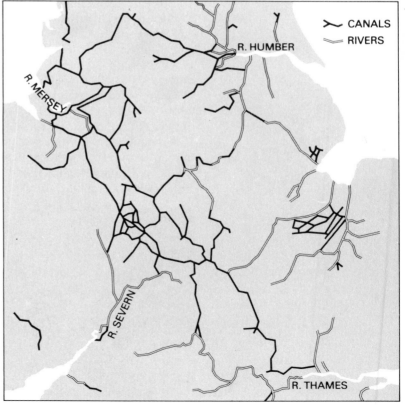

CANALS
RIVERS

R. HUMBER

R. MERSEY

R. SEVERN

R. THAMES

Q1 Why is transport by water cheaper than other methods?
Q2 Why has England an extensive network of canals?
Q3 Name the type of boat used on canals.
Q4 What are the main types of load carried by canal?
Q5 Who controls the canal system?
Q6 Name the four main estuaries linked by canal to the industrial Midlands.
Q7 Why is canal transport particularly slow?

Coastal Shipping

Coastal shipping transports goods from one port to another, using this cheap method for heavy loads e.g. coal from Newcastle to London; or bulky electrical generating machinery from South England to Scotland.

Traffic on "the narrow seas" round our coasts is particularly heavy. The English and Irish Channels are crossed by regular cargo lines, as well as ferries carrying vehicles and passengers.

Coastal freight is carried by private shippers.

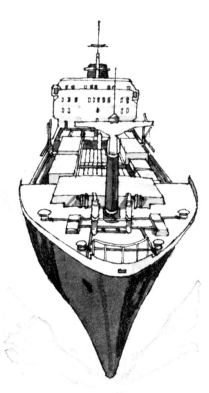

Ocean Shipping

Shipping **lines** follow regular routes between main world ports and run scheduled services of cargo ships as well as liners or passenger ships (which may also carry some cargo). Each Shipping Line or company publishes its own timetable or Shipping List.

A **Tramp**, by contrast, may be hired or chartered to sail anywhere required.

Some cargo ships carry mixed cargo in their holds, in bales, crates and containers. Others are specialised for a single cargo in bulk e.g. grain; or fruit or meat, in refrigerated holds; or oil or liquid gas, in tankers.

Q8 Why is the English Channel such a busy seaway?
Q9 Name three types of shipping that use these waters.
Q10 What type of goods are carried by coastal shipping? Give examples.
Q11 What is the difference between a liner and a tramp?
Q12 What is a Shipping List?
Q13 The size of cargo ships has increased in recent years. Name three types of bulk cargo carried.

Section 8

Ship owner   Cargo owner

BALTIC EXCHANGE

Ship   Chartering
broker   agent

The Baltic Exchange

A tramp may be hired, or chartered, to carry a cargo from, say, Liverpool to Buenos Aires. It will not then return empty, but will hope to pick up more business near Buenos Aires. Its next journey might be to Australia or back to Europe again.

The **Baltic Exchange** is the world market for the charter of ships (as well as for ship buying and ship repair). Here giant timetables show the booking dates and destinations of all tramp steamers in the world: so that someone wanting to charter a ship for cargo between Hong Kong and London, for instance, is able to find out what suitable ships will be in that part of the world at the right time.

All world shipowners have agents at the Baltic Exchange. Only Members of the Exchange may operate here, and these are either ship brokers or chartering agents. They represent either shipowners or cargo owners, who may be in different countries. Prices are agreed according to what ships are available at the time, and the charter or contract is drawn up.

The 'Baltic' originated in an eighteenth century coffee house where owners of ships and owners of cargoes got together. The Baltic Exchange also houses an international freight futures market and futures markets in grain, potatoes, soya bean meal an meat.

Shipper		

Shipper
LONGMAN GROUP LTD
FOURTH AVENUE
HARLOW
ESSEX

Consignee or order
PENGUIN BOOKS (AUSTRALIA) LTD
P O BOX 157
487-493 MAROONDAH HIGHWAY
AUSTRALIA

Notify party

Intended vessel and voyage number
JERVIS BAY   0106

Intended port of loading   TILBURY
Intended port of discharge   MELBOURNE

OCL SCNZ
AUSTRALIA/NEW ZEALAND SERVICE
NEW ZEALAND SERVICE

Bill of Lading no.   20519290.
Shipper's ref.   JOBS669670
OCL booking ref. no.   1285598

Bill of Lading for Combined Transport or Port to Port Shipment

CARRIER   OVERSEAS CONTAINERS LTD.

Accepted by the Carrier from the Shipper in apparent good order and condition (unless otherwise noted herein) the total numbers or quantity of containers or other packages or units indicated below ⊕ stated by the Shipper to comprise the cargo specified below, for transportation subject to all the terms hereof (including the terms on the reverse hereof and the terms of the Carrier's applicable tariff) from the place of acceptance or the port of loading, whichever applicable, to the port of discharge or the place of delivery, whichever applicable. On presentation of this document (duly endorsed) to the Carrier, by or on behalf of the Holder, the rights and liabilities arising in accordance with the terms hereof shall (without prejudice to any rule of common law or statute rendering them binding upon the Shipper, Holder and Carrier) become binding in all respects between the Carrier and Holder as though the contract contained herein or evidenced hereby had been made between them.

Freight and Charges
UK/Europe zone transport charge   PAID ORIGIN
UK/Europe port/LCL service charge
Ocean Freight   PAID ORIGIN
Destination port/LCL service charge
Destination zone transport charge   DUE DESTINATION

Details of cargo as declared by shipper

Marks and numbers	Quantity and type of package	Description of goods and container number Containers as indicated supplied by, or on behalf of the Carrier	Gross weight KILOS	Measurement CB.MS
P B MELBOURNE 669/1-13	13 PALET	CONTAINER NO. OCLU0210000 EDUCATIONAL PRINTED BOOKS	8200	12.883
P B FAIRFIELD MELBOURNE 670/1-9	9 PALET	CONTAINER NO. OCLU0210000 EDUCATIONAL PRINTED BOOKS AND AIDS	5370	8.515

Bill of Lading

A **Bill of Lading** is the document given by the Master of a ship to the cargo owner. It lists the goods accepted aboard; and states that they are in good condition (a clean bill) or with damaged packaging (a dirty bill).

At the destination, a copy of the Bill of Lading is presented by the importer to claim the goods at the dock side. If the cargo is sold by the owner while the goods are at sea, the Bill of Lading is handed to the new buyer as proof of the change of ownership. As a Bill of Lading is used as proof of ownership it is called a **Document of Title**.

Q1 What is the Baltic Exchange?
Q2 How does it help a cargo owner to arrange transport?
Q3 How does it help a shipowner to gain business?
Q4 Who are members operating at the Baltic Exchange?
Q5 What is a charter?
Q6 What other markets also operate at the Baltic Exchange?
Q7 What is a Bill of Lading?
Q8 What does it describe?
Q9 What is its use at the ship's destination?
Q10 Why is a Bill of Lading called a Document of Title?

Section 9

Goods transport (4)

By Air

Air transport of goods has grown faster than any other method over recent years. Not only is a plane the quickest means of transport, but goods are not shaken about and so need less packaging and insurance. This is a saving to set against the high freight charges.

Air transport has a particular advantage where goods are wanted quickly: emergency hospital supplies are rushed to an earthquake area; fashion goods fetch high prices if they are first in the shops; strawberries may be flown to London from California in December for expensive restaurants.

Air transport is not suitable for bulk loads of heavy goods, owing to the high cost, (though the carrying capacity of aircraft has increased steadily and they can now carry cars, tanks etc). However, a trader may choose to fly stocks to a shop in Canada, for example, and by quick response to orders save warehousing charges. The importer of a large computer may choose to have it flown in to enable this expensive piece of delicate machinery to be installed and put to work as soon as possible. Replacement parts may be flown, e.g. to Australia for a mining camp, where workers may be standing idle because of broken machinery.

Q1 What are the advantages of air transport for goods; and what is the main disadvantage?

Q2 Think of four examples where speed of transport is essential.

Q3 Think of four examples of loads for which air transport would not be suitable.

Q4 Give three examples of ways in which the high cost of air freight is partly off-set by other savings.

For speed, cargo is loaded in the airport warehouse on to wooden **pallets** or platforms in an igloo shape to match the inside of the plane. The pallets can then be driven out on to the runway and pushed from the back of the lorry directly into the plane.

British Airways has the widest network of freight lines in Europe. A number of air companies also compete for freight and charter work.

The Baltic Exchange became the main world Air Market for chartering planes (as it already had the know-how and experience of ship chartering). One of the main jobs of an air-agent or broker is to "fill the empty leg", i.e. to arrange a second cargo for the return leg of a journey, and thus be able to quote lower, more competitive rates for each trip. Aircraft, unlike ships, reckon to return to base between bookings.

An **Air Waybill** lists freight accepted for transport. It is not a "document of title" like a Bill of Lading but merely a receipt for goods taken aboard.

Q5 How is plane loading speeded?
Q6 Where is the world air market and what work is done there?
Q7 What is an Air Waybill?

Vocabulary

Air Waybill
Receipt for freight accepted for air transport.

Bill of Lading
This is a) a receipt for goods aboard ship
b) evidence of a contract for shipping the goods
and c) a "document of title" for ownership of
the goods.

Chartered
Hired transport under contract or charter.

Coastal Shipping
Ships sailing the narrow seas round Britain, e.g.
English and Irish Channels, and from port to
port around our coasts.

Commuters
Workers using rush-hour transport to and from
work.

Company train
British Rail rolling stock hired to transport
freight for a company, e.g. between its different
sites.

Consignment Note
A receipt for goods in transit by road or rail,
given to the consignor (sender).

Containers
Standard sized metal boxes in which goods are
packed for transport.

Container ports
Ports providing special cranes for the loading
and unloading of containers, with large parking
areas behind for stacking.

Container terminals
Rail/road junctions where special equipment is
provided for the speedy transfer of containers
betwen lorry and train.

Continental
Referring to the Continent of Europe.

Document of title
A form that is used as proof of ownership of
goods e.g. Bill of Lading.

Forwarding or Shipping Agents
Companies specialising in freight transport;
deciding on the best form of transport and
arranging the necessary documents.

Freight
Goods in transit, i.e. being transported. The
word "freight" is also used for the price charged
for transport.

Freightliners
All-container freight expresses.

Inter-City
Main line expresses travelling between large
towns.

Juggernauts
Very heavy articulated lorries with trailers often
coming over from the Continent on roll-on,
roll-off ferries.

Long distance haulage
Carriage of freight by road over long distances,
by transport companies or hauliers.

Pallet
Small wooden platform on to which goods are
loaded for mechanised quicker handling.

Roll-on, roll-off ferries
Ships used to transport passengers and vehicles,
and sometimes rail waggons.

Scheduled Line
A regular service on a fixed route with
timetabled stops.

Sealink
Ferry and hovercraft services linked to British
and French railways.

Tramp
Vessel hired or chartered to sail anywhere
required.

10 Credit

Credit buying enables people to enjoy the use of goods while they are still paying for them.

Different types of credit buying are arranged by retailers to suit customers: mail order credit, hire purchase (HP), monthly accounts etc. Credit means that the customer is, in effect, borrowing money. Finance Houses provide the funds necessary for hire purchase. Building Societies help house purchasers with long-term loans. These specialist organisations "buy" money by giving interest to savers, and "sell" money by charging a higher rate of interest to borrowers.

Sections
1. Credit   Monthly account   Budget account   Trading checks
2. Credit cards
3. Extended credit   Hire purchase   Hire Purchase Law
4. Financed sales   Finance Houses   Flat and true rate of interest
5. Building Societies

Section 1

Credit

"Credit" is given where full payment is not made immediately for a purchase. This may be looked upon as similar to borrowing money for a period, and just as interest is charged for a loan, so a credit charge is generally made. Some hire purchase or credit agreements cover months or years. No credit charge is usually made for short periods of a month or less. For example the milkman supplies milk which is not paid for until the end of the week. Newspapers are often delivered, and the bill is only settled weekly or monthly.

Monthly Account

A **Monthly Account** may be opened with a department store. Under this arrangement when goods are purchased no money changes hands, but the bill is signed by the customer. At the end of the month, a Statement is sent to the customer totalling her credit purchases and she then settles by cheque. No credit charge is made for monthly accounts.

Those wishing to make this arrangement with a department store must complete a form, give references, including a bank, and provide a specimen signature.

Q1 What is a credit purchase?
Q2 Give two examples of everyday credit sales where no credit charge is made.
Q3 Describe in your own words the monthly account system.
Q4 If you wanted to open a monthly account with a department store, what would you do?

Budget Account

Some credit arrangements depend on a regular payment by the customer of a fixed sum.

A **Budget Account** is common in clothes shops and department stores. The customer agrees a regular monthly or weekly payment, and the shops allow a credit limit related to this sum, e.g. 24 times the monthly payment. (A customer agrees to pay £5 a month, and a credit limit is granted of $24 \times £5 = £120$). The customer must continue to pay the agreed sum regularly, whether or not she has taken advantage of the credit available. This scheme is very useful for spreading the burden of expensive items, e.g. tailoring. A credit charge is made by the shop according to the amount of credit outstanding (unpaid) in any month.

Q5 If a shop allows a credit limit of 20 times the monthly payment agreed, what would be the credit limit allowed to a budget account customer paying £4 a month?
Q6 A customer has a budget account limit of £100 for a payment of £5 monthly, starting 1st June. On 15th June the customer buys a coat for £50 and on 26th June a blazer for £20. What would be

the outstanding credit balance on a) 28th June b) 3rd July; and for how much could the customer still make credit purchases at that shop on 3rd August?

Q7 For what type of purchases is a budget account common?

Trading Checks

These also provide credit against regular payments but allow it to be used in a number of shops. Regular payments are made to the representative of the **trading check** company, who calls at customers' homes. Checks or payment **vouchers** are given for 20 times the regular sum agreed. Repayment is made over 21 weeks, to include a credit charge. The vouchers may be spent at any shop in the scheme, which displays a sign, e.g. Provident. The shop sends the vouchers up to the trading check company and is paid by them.

Q8 Give two advantages to the customer of a trading check scheme.

Q9 How does the trading check company receive payment?

Q10 How is payment received by the shop where the credit purchases were made?

Section 2

Credit cards

Another type of credit buying is by **credit card**: the best known cards are Access and Barclaycard. Holders use their cards to purchase goods from shops; in restaurants; hotels; petrol stations; for rail and airline tickets; and for goods and services ordered by telephone. Some people have been round the world without cash in their pockets, using only credit cards for their fares, hotels, meals and other purchases! Retailers in a particular credit card scheme display the sign on their doors or windows.

When the customer makes a purchase, instead of paying immediately, she hands her credit card to the retailer, who places it under a roller to imprint its details on to slips, in triplicate (three carbons). The card is plastic and embossed with the customer's name and credit number, and carries her specimen signature. The roller machine also imprints the name and address of the shop on the slips, on which is written the price of the purchase. The customer then signs the slip in front of the shop assistant; and the signature should be compared with that on the credit card.

One copy of the slip is kept by the customer, and another by the shop. The third copy is presented for payment to a bank in that credit card scheme. By a special arrangement with the banks, they will credit immediately the account of the retailer presenting slips; and debit the account of the credit card company.

The retailer pays a Merchant Service charge monthly to the credit card company to meet their expenses. The system is still worthwhile to the retailer, although his profit is reduced, because it attracts customers who might not otherwise have the money for the purchase.

Q1 Give the names of two credit cards.
Q2 How does a credit card holder know if a retailer will accept his card?
Q3 What information is contained on a credit card, and why?
Q4 How does the shop receive payment for the goods sold?

The card holder receives from the credit card company a statement every month, listing all his credit purchases during the previous month. If the total outstanding amount is paid before the date given (often as long as 25 days is allowed), no credit charge is made. But if payment is delayed for longer than this period, interest is charged for the loan. Some payment, say 5 percent, must be made every month; but any balance unpaid, plus interest, is carried forward to the next month's statement. Each credit card holder is given a credit limit, and is not allowed to go beyond this.

Some credit cards may be used to withdraw money from cash dispensers e.g. Access cards may be used on Cashline machines, with a secret personal number that the card holder keys into the machine. Up to £100 a day may be withdrawn. Larger amounts may be withdrawn against a credit card by going in to a bank – provided you stay within your credit limit! This is a great convenience for people when not near their home branch to withdraw money. For

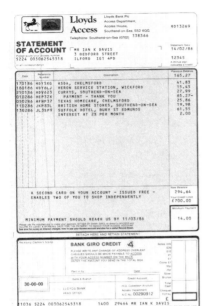

this service, they are charged interest from the date of the cash withdrawal.

In the future credit cards will be used in machines to purchase a wide range of goods. Railway tickets and petrol can already be purchased in this way, under the PIN scheme – Personal Identification Number.

Credit cards are not run by banks, but by separate credit card companies often linked to banks e.g. Barclaycard is linked to Barclays; Access is linked to Lloyds, Midland, National Westminster and others. Payment by a card holder is made to the credit company: amounts due cannot be deducted by a bank straight from a customer's account. Someone may hold a credit card not linked to her own bank, e.g. a National Westminster account holder may hold a Barclaycard.

The large credit card companies have expanded and developed their systems all over the world, under such names as **Visa** or **Mastercard**. Credit card purchases can be made abroad as easily as in your home country.

Charge cards, such as American Express and Diners Club, similarly allow for purchases against a plastic card: but each monthly statement must be settled in full.

Cards are easily stolen and used fraudulently: so they should be looked after carefully. If missing, the card number should be immediately reported to the credit card company by telephone, at any time of the day or night. The customer may be liable to pay something if the card is wrongly used by someone else for purchases before it is reported. Holographs on credit cards guard against forgery of cards.

Q5 Imagine that you are explaining the credit card system to a friend. What should you tell her about the monthly statement?
Q6 What is the main disadvantage of getting cash on a credit card?
Q7 Who run credit card schemes?
Q8 What does PIN stand for, and how is it used?
Q9 Discuss whether the use of credit cards could make cash unnecessary, or in what circumstances cash is still more convenient.

Section 3

For large purchases, e.g. furniture, it is common to pay a deposit and then monthly instalments until the full cost plus a credit charge has been paid.

Extended credit

Extended credit describes a purchase where the goods become the property of the buyer immediately (as with monthly accounts, budget accounts, mail order or trading check purchases).

Hire purchase

Hire purchase (HP), on the other hand, describes a scheme whereby the goods are **hired** until the full payment has been completed. Only then does the purchaser become the real owner of the goods he has been using. He may not resell the goods that are still under a Hire Purchase agreement as they do not belong to him.

Non-Payment
If instalments are not kept up under an extended credit agreement, the buyer may be taken to Court for debt. On the other hand, if HP instalments are not kept up, the company, who still own the goods, may sometimes take them back (repossess them).

Contracts
For all hire purchase arrangements a **contract** is signed, as well as for extended credit sales over £50. The contract sets out the conditions of the agreement, and is signed by both the customer and the company. A copy is kept by each.

Q1 For large purchases, what is the common repayment pattern?
Q2 What is meant by an extended credit purchase?
Q3 What is meant by hire purchase?
Q4 Why may goods under hire purchase not be resold?
Q5 What happens if instalments are not kept up under
   a) an extended credit agreement
   b) a hire purchase agreement?

Hire purchase law

Under the law every hire purchase or extended credit **agreement** must set out the cash price of the goods, the amount and number of **instalments** and the total amount to be paid. When an agreement is signed in a shop, the buyer is bound by the contract. Under an extended credit agreement, the goods belong to the buyer immediately and he is responsible for paying the full amount. Under an HP agreement, however, he has the right to stop hiring the goods.

Beside the space where the customer signs the HP agreement, there must be a red-framed box telling him that he has the right to end it. But he should read the agreement carefully to see the conditions he is bound by! The customer must pay the full number of instalments for the months the goods have been used. And, because after use the goods are secondhand, the customer has to pay at least half the HP price.

If the customer has paid more than one-third of the full price and then falls behind with instalments, the company must obtain a Court Order before repossessing the goods. The Court will always try to help someone who is honest but is having difficulty with repayments, e.g. by arranging reduced instalments over a longer period.

Because a housewife alone in the house may sometimes sign an agreement for a persuasive doorstep sales representative which she later regrets, the law lays down special protection whenever the contract is signed outside the shop. The customer must receive a copy of the agreement within seven days and then has a five day "cooling-off" period in which she may cancel the agreement, in writing.

Q6 What details of payment must be set out in an agreement?
Q7 How is the attention of the signer drawn to her right to end an HP agreement?
Q8 What minimum payment must be made if an HP agreement is ended before time?
Q9 Where instalments have not been kept up, what is a limit on the right of the HP company to repossess the goods?
Q10 How may the Court help an honest person in difficulties with payment of instalments due?
Q11 What is the purpose of the "cooling-off period" for doorstep agreements?

Section 4 — Financed sales

Most shops (except department stores) cannot afford to finance their own HP, i.e. to wait months for payment. They therefore turn for help to a Finance House.

1 The shop supplies the goods to the customer and makes a profit from the sale;
2 the shop is paid straight away by the Finance House;
3 the Finance House is repaid over a period by the customer. Instalments cover both the cash price and a credit charge. This credit charge is the profit of the Finance House.

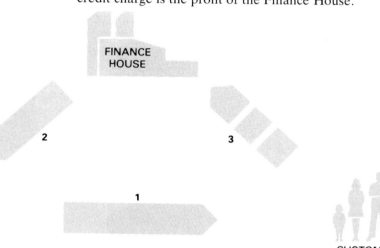

The HP contract is between the customer and the Finance House, even though the agreement is signed in the shop, and instalments may be paid to the shop.

The same applies to extended credit agreements.

Q1 Why are Finance Houses brought in on large credit sales by shops?
Q2 What are the advantages of this arrangement to the shop?
Q3 What are the advantages to the customer?
Q4 What are the advantages to the Finance House?
Q5 Where is the contract made and completed between the Finance House and the customer?

Finance Houses

The money supply of a Finance House comes from
a) shareholders
b) bank loans
c) depositors.

The Finance House advertises for deposits by offering a high rate of interest to anyone who will leave with them a large sum over a period (e.g. £300 for three years).

They use their funds to finance HP sales in shops; the hiring or leasing of machinery and equipment by industry; vehicle purchases etc.

They charge customers a higher rate of interest than they offer to depositors. The difference between the price at which they "buy" money and at which they "sell" money covers their administrative expenses, or running costs, and their profit. Since a high rate of interest is paid to depositors to attract large sums which may be used over a period, it follows that the credit charge to customers will be even higher.

Thus a hire purchase arrangement with a Finance House is not a cheap way of "buying" credit.

Q6 From where does a Finance House obtain funds?

Q7 Why might someone deposit with a Finance House instead of with a bank?

Q8 What type of deposit is a Finance House interested in?

Q9 How are Finance House funds used?

Q10 What is meant by saying that Finance Houses "buy" and "sell" money?

SHAREHOLDERS   BANK LOANS   DEPOSITORS

FINANCE HOUSE

HIRE PURCHASE, LEASING, RENTING OF EQUIPMENT AND PREMISES

REPAYMENTS, INCLUDING CREDIT CHARGE

Flat and True Rate of Interest

If you borrow £100, and repay £108 a year later, the rate of interest is 8 per cent per annum. However, you may pay back the sum by 12 monthly instalments of £9. Then, only £91 was owed after one month, only £82 after two months. After 11 months, only £9 was still owed. If 8 per cent had been calculated on the reducing sum each month (e.g. 8 per cent of £91 the second month; 8 per cent of £82 the third month), you would only have had to repay about £104. £108 would represent about 16 per cent on 12 monthly instalments. A flat rate (8%) may roughly be doubled to give a picture of the true rate of interest, where a loan is repaid by instalments.

Q11 If you borrow £200 at 10 per cent per annum for two years, what total would you pay at the end of the period?

Q12 If you repaid the above loan by monthly instalments, what would be your true rate of interest, approximately?

Section 5

Building societies

Building Societies exist to aid people to buy their own homes. This involves such a large outlay of money that few people would ever afford it without credit. In this case the credit is supplied by the Building Society with a **mortgage.**

The house buyer becomes the owner of the property, and his/her name is entered on the **Deeds of the house**, which is the legal claim to ownership. The buyer pays the seller a deposit, and then the remainder of the purchase price is paid to the seller by the Building Society. For the long period of repayment of this loan — often 25 years — the Building Society hold the Deeds of the house, so that it cannot be resold without their permission while it is still under mortgage. The value of the property itself guarantees that the Building Society's loan will be repaid.

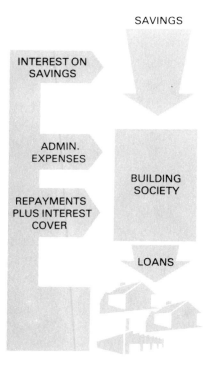

SAVINGS

INTEREST ON SAVINGS

ADMIN. EXPENSES

BUILDING SOCIETY

REPAYMENTS PLUS INTEREST COVER

LOANS

When the mortgage has finally been fully paid off — not only the sum borrowed but the interest on it — then the Deeds are returned to the owner. Mortgages apply to property of all kinds — flats, houses, shops, factories, offices, etc.

Q1 What do Building Societies exist to do?

Q2 Why do so many people turn to Building Societies for help?

Q3 a) What legal document changes hands when a house is bought?

b) What part does this document play in a mortgage?

Q4 Describe the steps taken by the buyer in paying the purchase price of a house with a mortgage. What is added to this price?

Q5 For what besides houses are mortgages suitable?

Saving with a building society

From where do Building Societies get the funds to lend to property purchasers? They have become one of the largest "collectors of savings" in the country by offering good interest rates to savers. There are always so many people coming to Building Societies for help, newly weds etc, that Building Societies make sure of a steady in-flow of savings by offering attractive rates of interest. Different types of account are available, for casual savers or for regular savers. They run a number of branch offices, and make it easy for people to withdraw their savings when they choose.

All savers become members of the Society. If there are more applications for loans than the Building Society can satisfy, it will give priority to members, i.e. it will give mortgages to people who have already saved with it.

The government allows tax relief, or refund, on mortgage repayment interest each year, and this is a help to house buyers.

Q6 "A Building Society is both a lender and a borrower". Explain this.

Q7 People are always wanting money for house purchases. How do Building Societies make sure of a steady flow of savings in to them?

Q8 Who are the members of a Building Society and what advantages do they receive?

Q9 How does the government help people to buy their own homes?

Q10 What do mortgage repayments have to cover? The diagram will help you.

ARE YOU WITH THE WINNERS?

YES, WE'RE WITH THE WOOLWICH!

The safe place, with the nice face.

W
WOOLWICH
EQUITABLE BUILDING SOCIETY

Get the Abbey Habit

HERTS AND ESSEX BUILDING SOCIETY

Nationwide
Building Society

Vocabulary

Agreement
A printed contract setting out the details of an extended credit sale or hire purchase.

Budget account
Credit arrangement whereby the customer makes a regular monthly payment which decides the credit limit (e.g. 20 × the monthly payment).

Deeds of a house
The legal document showing ownership.

Extended credit
Buyer pays a deposit and then monthly instalments; the goods become his/her property immediately.

Finance House
An organisation financing credit.

Flat rate (of interest)
The rate quoted for a loan or credit as if repayment were at the end of the period (rather than by instalments).

Hire Purchase
Deposit plus instalments paid for the use of goods, which do not become the property of the hirer until the final payment.

Monthly account
Credit arrangement whereby the customer does not pay at once for the goods but signs the bill. A monthly statement is sent by the shop showing the total owed, which must then be paid.

Mortgage
Loan for the purchase of property, using the ownership deeds as guarantee of repayment.

Trading Checks
Payment vouchers issued by a Trading Check company for use in shops in the scheme. The customer pays a regular amount each week to the representative of the Trading Check company.

True rate (of interest)
The real percentage paid on a loan reduced by monthly instalments.

11 Advertising

Advertising is a part of our everyday lives. We rely on it for much information: and take pleasure in its brightness, its decorativeness, ingenuity and humour.

However, we must realise that the aim of advertising is to sell a product or service. The cleverness used by advertisers may be directed at influencing the consumer, rather than informing him. At its worst, it plays on emotions and has little to do with the value or quality of the product.

The consumer must learn to "see through" advertising, and use it rather than letting it use him.

Sections

Section 1

The aims of advertising

We are surrounded by advertising everywhere we go. We see it every day, in the streets, when travelling, in newspapers and magazines, and on radio and television. We are the target of advertising from the time we are children.

The object of advertising is to inform and to persuade people. Advertising tells you about events (e.g. jumble sales); about products and services available (e.g. new wristwatch, 24-hour cleaning); about prices (e.g. bargain mid-week fares). Some advertising is only to inform people (e.g. pensioners' holidays available) or to educate them (e.g. "Guard that Fire!") but most advertising is done by firms to persuade people to buy their goods.

The advertising industry continually tries to think up new and attractive ideas for selling products. They judge their success on how much they succeed in raising the sales of that product, rather than on whether the product is good value for money. Some successful advertising campaigns have been run on products which may be actually harmful. It is therefore up to consumers not to be easily influenced to part with their money. Advertising does much to brighten our lives: but there are dangers as well as advantages.

Q1 Think of and list 10 ways of advertising.

Q2 Describe four advertisements aimed at children of different ages.

Q3 Discuss two advertisements that you find particularly attractive, and the reasons why.

Q4 What makes an advertising campaign a success?

Q5 Mention two products widely advertised that might be harmful to people.

Q6 Give two ways in which advertising brightens our lives; and two situations in which it might be resented.

Q7 Design a packet for a new breakfast cereal called "Crunchies", thinking carefully about
  a) who is most likely to eat it
  b) who is most likely to buy it
  c) what slogans are most likely to influence sales.

Advertising agencies

A company must decide how much it is prepared to spend in a year on advertising. If it is advertising widely it will generally employ an **advertising agency** to plan a campaign. They will decide where the advertising should be placed to get the best results for money and what form it should take. They may arrange **market research** to find out who are most likely to buy the product (men or women, what age group, what income group, etc). They then aim the advertising to attract this group of people. Hundreds of thousands of pounds are spent on advertising "wars" between rival companies selling similar products.

The most expensive form of advertising is the television commercial because it reaches the largest number of people. The cost increases with the length of the commercial and peak viewing times. Similarly, a newspaper or magazine will charge for each column centimetre of advertising, according to the size of its circulation or readership, and also according to the position of the advertisement.

There are many specialist magazines dealing with interests or hobbies; and trade journals for different types of business.

Q8 In what publications would you place the following advertisements:
  a) a special offer for a summer dress for the 15–20 year old, direct from the warehouse
  b) family camping equipment
  c) national supermarket offer of cheap Cheddar cheese
  d) a jumble sale
  e) post of receptionist in a hotel
  f) restaurant kitchen equipment?

Q9 How are advertising campaigns planned?

Q10 Who, in the long run, pays for advertising?

Q11 a) Why is the television commercial the most expensive form of advertising?
  b) What influences the cost of the commercial?

Q12 A central London department store wishes to place a 10 cm, three-column advertisement for its Sale. For one cm deep per single column, the "City Times" charge £20.00; the "Morning Standard" charge £16.50; and the "Weekly Telegraph" charge £25.00. Calculate the cost of the desired advertisement, in each paper, and give arguments that might influence the choice between them.

Section 2

Persuasion

Manufacturers' market research may benefit the consumer by consulting what people like and dislike. However, much advertising is cleverly aimed at capturing the shoppers' interest in a way that has little to do with the product. For example, puppies or pretty girls may be used in an advertisement to draw your attention, whatever the product. Emotions may be worked on to promote sales.

Sex is the interest most frequently exploited; for example, a girl in a bikini may be sitting on top of a new car model on display.

"Snob-appeal" is used in advertisements that show a luxurious life-style, or what the "best people" do.

The desire for beauty is used to lure people into buying a great range of products, e.g. cosmetics.

Adventure and romance (however unlikely) are dramatised to remain in the customer's mind, linked with the name of the product.

Fears are played on, as regards bodily hygiene, e.g. in deodorant advertisements.

Natural parental feelings are roused, with pictures of children and happy family life, to boost sales of toys, detergents etc.

All these appeals to emotion encourage shoppers to buy, buy, buy — whether or not they really need the goods and with little reference to the worth of the product.

Q1 List five emotions which are frequently exploited by advertisers.
Q2 Describe in detail an advertisement using adventure or romance to raise the appeal of a product.
Q3 List three products often sold because the customer has hopes of becoming more beautiful by using the product.
Q4 A number of advertisements play on doubts and hopes about being attractive to the opposite sex. Describe one of these.
Q5 "Advertising is used to create a demand for a product." What is meant by "creating a demand"?

Common-Sense in Looking at Advertising

No matter how attractive an advertisement is, consumers should not allow their emotions to be captured by skilful presentation, so that the advertiser succeeds in making them part with their money for the wrong reasons.

Common-sense is necessary in facing advertisers' suggestions. No washing powder can make garments "whiter than white": the phrase is meaningless. No soap can make someone beautiful. Whether one person is attracted to another does not depend on the brand of their perfume.

Real information should be looked for in an advertisement, and what advantages of a product make it a sensible purchase.

Q6 What three pieces of common-sense advice would you give on viewing advertisements?

Q7 Look at all the advertisements shown on both pages and comment on each one, discussing the emotions appealed to, and the amount of actual information given.

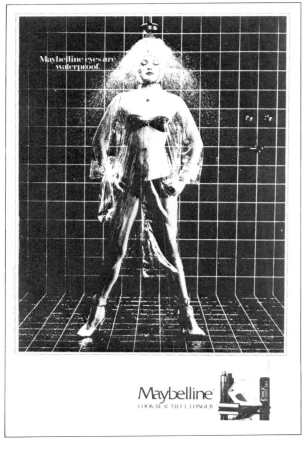

Section 3

Official control of advertising

Control, by law, of advertisements which may mislead or may be harmful has been found necessary.

The Trades Descriptions Act bans "false and misleading" statements. For example, an hotel may not advertise "sea view" if the sea can only be seen from the roof with binoculars!

A claim in patent medicine advertisements to "cure" diseases is banned by law.

The Independent Broadcasting Authority (IBA), through their advertising advisory committee, supervises and controls advertisements broadcast on television and radio. Their printed Code of Practice does not allow advertisements of cigarettes, or of products that might give offence. No food or drink advertisement may claim to lead to weight reduction by itself. This statement is untrue of any product, unless combined with a controlled diet. Some advertisements try to get round this by saying that anyone using their product will "lose inches".

When children are likely to be watching, advertisements must not show scenes that might be dangerous for them, e.g. climbing drainpipes. Also, children must not be made to feel that they are failing in loyalty or duty by not doing something, (e.g. buying a present for Mother's Day); and they must not be encouraged by the advertisement to nag parents for products.

Q1 Why have laws been passed controlling claims in advertisements?
Q2 How do the IBA control advertisements?
Q3 Why may no food or drink advertisement claim to reduce weight by itself?
Q4 Give three examples of advertisements affecting children that are considered undesirable.

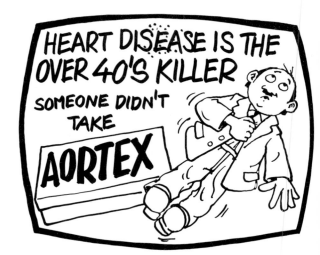

Voluntary control of advertising

The advertising industry itself has drawn up the British Code of Advertising Practice. This Code lays down that advertisements should not play on fear, and that certain diseases, such as cancer and ulcers, should not be mentioned.

Q5 What voluntary code tries to maintain standards in advertising?

Q6 Give two examples of this code as it affects health.

Q7 Give reasons why the advertisements below would be disapproved of?

    a) "Viruseen will cure your cold."

    b) A child, in a brand of tough shoes, seen balancing on a high wall.

    c) "Do you love your mother? Have you bought her a box of Caring Candies for Mother's Day?"

    d) "Do others admire you at school? Are you wearing the new Space Age jacket? Get your Mother to buy you one now!"

Q8 Comment on whether the advertisements below on both pages should be allowed and give your reasons.

Section 4

Market research

In order to sell as much as possible, manufacturers will often undertake market research before starting mass production on a new line, to find out what the consumer likes best. They may have several samples tested by a variety of consumers, and note their responses. For example, furniture polishes may be tested by housewives to see if they prefer a lavender or pine scent, or no smell, to their polish. Shoppers may be asked to taste different blends of salad cream, to choose the flavour preferred. Not only taste, but appearance, label design, colour and packaging are also tested to see which attracts consumers most. Questionnaires on existing goods or services are used to check customer reaction, e.g. on service provided by an airline.

Q1 What is market research?
Q2 Describe an example of market research.
Q3 What features of a product may be tested for consumer preference?

Sales promotion

Besides advertising, many gimmicks are used to boost or promote sales: gifts and offers; competitions; coupons; prizes; special displays; tasting or testing samples; decorative packaging. Most sales promotion is arranged by **manufacturers** for their branded goods.

Q4 List five types of sales promotion.
Q5 Describe three different types of special offer which might be used to increase sales.

WHSMITH

Branding

A brand name or symbol enables a manufacturer to advertise his products. He is able to reach the customer direct by advertising, rather than having to rely on displays by wholesalers or retailers. The shopper selects goods by name, e.g. *Heinz* beans, *Typhoo* tea. Very often "consumer loyalty" is built up so that a shopper chooses goods of the same brand as another product liked, e.g. a customer who enjoys *Libbys* peaches may choose *Libbys* rice pudding.

The competition between some brands, e.g. washing powders, is so fierce that advertising "wars" cost many hundreds of thousands of pounds.

Most branding is done by manufacturers. However, with the rise of very large retailing chains, orders in bulk are placed direct with manufacturers by the chain, e.g. Tesco or Marks and Spencer, and by arrangement the goods are packaged under the retailer's brand. These "**own brands**" can be sold at lower prices than the manufacturer's brands because the wholesaler is cut out. The large retail chains do not rely on advertising to sell their "own brands" but confidently expect their customers to select their cheaper brand.

Q6 What is the advantage of branding a product?
Q7 Give three examples of **manufacturers'** brand names in grocery products and three in cars.
Q8 Give three examples of brand names used by chain retailers.
Q9 Give the names of rivals in a serice where suppliers advertise in competition with each other.
Q10 Give two reasons why "own brands" are cheaper than manufacturers' brands.

Vocabulary

Advertising agency
A firm specialising in advertising — advising, designing, writing, filming; and placing advertisements to best advantage, for the money available.

Brand
A distinctive trademark (a name or symbol).

Code of Practice
Printed rules governing behaviour, e.g. rules controlling advertising.

Market research
Research aimed at finding out consumer spending patterns, their likes and dislikes.

Sales promotion
Methods of encouraging sales, e.g. special offers.

12 Consumer protection

A shopper can often not judge the quality of manufactured goods without expert advice from sales staff, e.g. on mattresses or carpets. It is impossible to see the inside of many products or for the ordinary person to judge if they will wear well. The need for standards to be established and for information to be given to the consumer has been increasingly recognised in recent years. This is known as **Consumer Protection.** Consumers have set up their own organisations to give advice and do research, and the number of laws controlling production and selling is growing.

Careful shoppers should know something of their rights; of where to turn for help and advice, and of how to go about getting complaints looked into and put right.

Sections
1. Manufacturers' standards   British Standards Institution
   Design Centre
2. Wise shopping   The Consumers' Association
   Local consumer advice
3. Consumer law (1)
4. Contracts   Guarantees
5. Consumer law (2)
6. Complaints

Section 1

Certification Trade Mark

Pure new wool

The International Wool Secretariat only allow their **Woolmark** symbol to be used with goods made from 100% pure new wool.

British Electro-Technical Approvals Board (BEAB) guarantees an internationally agreed level of safety for electrical appliances.

The Association of British Travel Agents members agree to abide by a special code of practice.

Manufacturers' standards

A shopper may be deceived by attractive-looking goods which are, in fact, of poor quality. However, many manufacturers are concerned to keep up the standard of goods they produce. A manufacturer may do research, testing and quality control on his production line. Some give guarantees with goods, of quality and safety. Many label goods carefully to inform the shopper about materials used, washing instructions etc. Goods under a particular brand or symbol are of a uniform quality.

Sometimes organisations or unions of manufacturers lay down a set of rules or good standards for a particular trade, which their members agree to follow.

Q1 Give three examples of pre-packed goods where it is not possible to judge the contents when buying.

Q2 Name three products on which a careful shopper would expect to get advice when buying.

Q3 How may a manufacturer help the shopper to be informed about a garment?

Q4 How do manufacturers maintain the quality of branded goods?

Q5 a) What does the "Woolmark" mean?
b) Give three products on which you might look for the "Woolmark"?

Q6 a) What is the advantage of buying goods with the BEAB label?
b) Give three examples of equipment that might qualify.

Q7 Holidaymakers on package holidays abroad have been known to find half-built hotels or over-booked rooms. How may people guard against such disappointments?

WHAT A LOVELY CHEAP BLANKET!

BLANKETS SALE

SOMETIMES THEY ARE MADE FROM RE-USED WOOL. HAS IT GOT THE WOOLMARK?

I GOT A SHOCK OFF THIS!

YOU SHOULD HAVE MADE SURE IT HAD THE BEAB LABEL WHEN YOU BOUGHT IT.

British Standards Institution

The **British Standards Institution** (BSI) is a body which lays down desirable standards of manufacture for a great range of goods. Any manufacturer may submit his products for inspection and thereafter have the right to attach the Kitemark, certifying BSI standards.

The BSI co-operate with similar foreign organisations to achieve accepted international standards and symbols. Washing and cleaning symbols have been internationally agreed, for example.

The Design Centre

The Design Council aims to encourage the production of goods that are efficiently designed for their purpose and beautiful to look at. Products that have received their award may carry the **Design Centre** label. All such products are catalogued at the Design Centre, London, where displays are held.

Q8 Draw the Kitemark and say what it guarantees.

Q9 Draw the Design Council award label and say why products may carry it.

Washing machine setting and temperature of water

Dry-cleanable

Iron temperature setting

Section 2

Wise shopping

The wise shopper will inspect goods carefully as far as possible. For example, on a garment are the seams well stitched; are there spare matching buttons; and are the hems generous on children's clothes to allow for letting down? Are there washing or cleaning instructions? On electrical goods, do labels show that safety has been specially tested? Is after-sales service available, and mechanical spare parts?

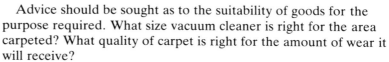

Advice should be sought as to the suitability of goods for the purpose required. What size vacuum cleaner is right for the area carpeted? What quality of carpet is right for the amount of wear it will receive?

Q1 What points would a wise shopper consider when buying:
    a) a child's winter coat
    b) wall paper
    c) a shirt in a man-made fibre?
Q2 Discuss three goods where after-sales service and spares availability are important.

The Consumers' Association

Choice of goods bought may depend on personal taste but organisations have been set up to provide useful information for shoppers. Newspapers and magazines sometimes provide shopping news and advice. The **Consumers' Association** publishes a monthly magazine for members called '*Which*'. In each issue different types of goods are discussed and, for each, several brands are tested and compared for price, performance and quality. Shoppers are told what points to watch out for, and what tests have been made. A "Best Buy" for each type of good spotlights value-for-money. To ensure that they are entirely independent and uninfluenced, '*Which*' accepts no manufacturers' advertisements and goods for testing are bought in shops anonymously.

The Consumers' Association have established a wide reputation. Their advice is sought by official bodies as standing for the interests of consumers. They are quoted on radio and television. Anyone can become a member and receive 'Which' and their other magazines on holidays, and gardening, or buy pamphlets which they publish.

Q3 What is 'Which'?

Q4 What are 'Which' articles concerned with?

Q5 How do the Consumers' Association ensure that their published views are independent of manufacturers?

Local consumer advice

Local **Consumer Groups** have meetings of members interested in consumer affairs and produce shopping information for the locality. Annual conferences are held by the National Association of Consumer Groups.

Consumer interests are now taken so seriously that the government and local authorities have helped in the setting up of centres where shoppers can get help and advice. **Consumer Advice Centres** do local retail surveys, and stock a large number of pamphlets telling shoppers their rights under the law; and give help and advice. **Citizens' Advice Bureaux** advise on a much wider range of problems than just shopping ones, e.g. on housing, legal matters, social problems.

If a shopper has a grievance against a supplier, either of these organisations will advise on the right steps to take.

The **Office of Fair Trading** is a government department concerned with fair trading and Codes of Practice; and with enforcing consumer law. The **National Consumer Council** watches over consumer affairs and advises the government.

Q6 What is a Consumer Group?

Q7 What is a Consumer Advice Centre?

Q8 How does a Citizens' Advice Bureau differ from a Consumer Advice Centre?

Section 3

Consumer law (1)

A number of laws now protect the shopper against bad trading practices. These laws are enforced by local inspectors called **Trading Standards Officers** employed at the Town Hall. The local Health Department will also inspect premises, and may follow up shoppers' complaints. Shoppers should know their rights under different laws.

Food and Drugs Act (1955) makes it an offence to sell food in dirty or unhygienic premises. Unfit food may not be sold, e.g. horse meat is listed for sale as animal food, but not for human consumption. It is also an offence to describe food in a false or misleading way, e.g. "raspberry" jam must contain a given proportion of real raspberries. There are many regulations controlling the sale of drugs.

The local **Environmental Health Office** wish to know about any cases of suspected food poisoning so that they can trace the source, and prevent others being affected.

Weights and Measures Act (1963) lays down that with pre-packed food and household products the net weight or quantity must be shown. Certain standard common foods such as tea, milk, sugar and butter may only be packed in standard sizes or weights. Trading Standards Officers visit traders to check weighing machines, measures, etc.

Labelling of Food Regulations (1970) state that pre-packed foods must show on the label a list of the ingredients used. A brand name must also be described in easily understood words, e.g. "Whipseasy — quick setting blancmange".

Q1 Peter was sure that the amount of froth on his beer concealed the fact that he was not getting a full pint measure from the new publican. Which law should he know about, and what should he do?

Q2 Sandra is going on a diet and wishes to check whether a tin of orange juice is natural or contains added sugar. The label gives no information. What law should she know about, and what should she do?

Q3 Mary bought some cooked meat from the supermarket. When she unwrapped it for her lunch, it smelt so bad that she did not eat it. What law should she know about, and what should she do?

Q4 Sally bought four metres of gingham material to make a summer dress but found that by her tape measure the length was short. She took it back to the shop and they again measured the length with the same result. Which law should she know about, and what should she do if she is not satisfied?

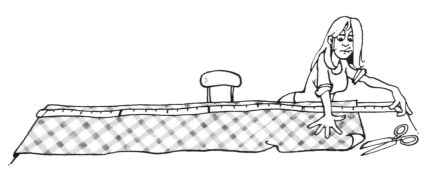

Section 4

Contracts

A **contract** is any agreement between a buyer and a seller for the sale of either goods or services. The contract is binding in law, and if it is broken a court may grant compensation.

Contracts need not only be **written**, but may be **verbal** or spoken.

There must be an **offer** (to pay), and then an **acceptance** of the offer, for a contract to be made. For example, if you buy a ticket for a pop concert, there is a contract to provide a show for you in exchange for your payment. If the show is cancelled you get your money back.

In a contract, **each side** promises to do something for the other, e.g. one side promises to pay, and the other side promises to provide goods or services. A gift is one-sided, and so a contract is not involved.

When you buy goods in a shop, it is the buyer who is making the offer (of money), and the shop who may agree to sell or not. In a supermarket an offer has not been made until the customer reaches the check-out point. If a telephone order for goods has been accepted, a contract has been made.

Q1 What is a contract?

Q2 What happens if a contract is broken?

Q3 Do all contracts have to be signed?

Q4 When has a contract been made?

Q5 If your uncle promises to buy you a tape recorder and then does not, has he broken a contract?

Q6 Has a contract been made
- a) if you buy a newspaper?
- b) if you take a scarf to the shop window to match colours in daylight?
- c) if you put goods in to a supermarket trolley?
- d) if you order goods by telephone?

Q7 In the three pictures opposite, explain in each case whether a contract has been broken or not.

Guarantees

A sale of goods is on the understanding that the article will last for a reasonable time without repair, e.g. a year for electrical hardware. If the goods do not last a reasonable time, the seller is responsible for giving compensation, or replacement, or free repair.

Sometimes the manufacturer will print a card or label stating the terms of his guarantee. However, even if the buyer does not "sign and return" a guarantee card, he still has his rights. If the guarantee makes a better-than-average offer, e.g. for five years instead of the usual one year, then this is binding on the manufacturer.

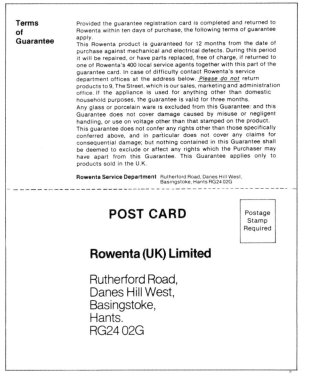

Q8 What rights has the buyer if goods do not last a reasonable time?

Q9 What information is requested on a guarantee card? Discuss the position of a buyer who has not returned this card.

Q10 Has a binding contract been made if a manufacturer offers better-than-average terms in a printed guarantee?

Section 5

Consumer law (2)

Sale of Goods Act (1979) — lays down that goods sold must be of a quality fit for their normal purpose. This is called **merchantable quality.** If the customer states a special purpose for which they want to buy the goods, then the article sold must be fit for that special purpose. If the goods are described, e.g. in an advertisement, the goods sold must match the description exactly. If the goods are faulty the customer has the right to choose a cash refund, or accept replacement or repair. The **Supply of Goods and Services Act** (1982) extends similar protection to the consumer of services and repairs.

Trade Descriptions Act (1968) — makes it a criminal offence for a trader to describe goods or services falsely, whether in words or by a picture.

If "Sale" goods are described as "Reduced", they must have been on sale at the higher price in that shop for at least one month in the last six months. Otherwise, Sale bargains may only be described as "Special Purchases".

Unsolicited Goods and Services Act (1971) — refers to goods sent to people's homes that they never ordered. Later, payment is demanded for the goods; but the Act now makes this illegal. The householder may do one of two things; either keep the goods safe for six months, or write to the sender asking for the goods to be collected and allow 30 days. After this time the householder is free to keep or dispose of the goods.

Q1 Richard was pleased with his gleaming new refrigerator — until, only a month after he had bought it, the door handle came adrift. Had the law been broken and, if so, how and under which Act of Parliament?

Q2 Mary told the shop assistant that she wanted a vacuum cleaner for a three storey house with fitted carpets. Nine months later her repairer told her that this model was too small for the amount of carpet in the house.

Had the law been broken, and, if so how, and under which Act of Parliament?

Q3 John and Sara booked a holiday in Cornwall at a caravan site advertised as "only 50 yards from the sea". They found that the site was on top of a cliff and it took 15 minutes to reach the beach.

Had the law been broken and, if so how, and under which Act of Parliament?

Q4 Malcolm had an unexpected parcel delivered and found it contained an illustrated Wildlife manual. The accompanying letter said that the book was on 15 days' approval, and if not returned in that time, the publishers would assume that he wanted to keep the goods and pay for them.

Must Malcolm do as they say? What are his rights under the law?

Section 6

Complaints

There are many occasions on which someone is dissatisfied with a purchase. Sometimes you buy goods on the spur of the moment and regret it later. A pair of shoes may never feel comfortable even after weeks of "wearing in"! This is either bad luck or bad judgement when shopping. The only advice here is always to think carefully and always to examine the goods thoroughly before buying. However, sometimes the goods themselves are faulty and the shopper has grounds for complaint. The goods should then be taken back to the shop, and the situation explained. Do not try home repairs.

In law (**Sale of Goods Act**) the shopkeeper has a duty to sell only goods of "merchantable quality". The fault may lie in the manufacture of the goods, but it is up to the **shopkeeper** to take this up with the manufacturer after the customer has been satisfied.

Shopkeepers will generally accept a politely expressed complaint — but only, of course, for goods sold by them. It is therefore most important to keep bills and receipts carefully as proof of the place and date of purchase. The customer has the right to choose between a refund, or alternate goods, or repairs. You need not accept a credit note, and can insist on cash for the faulty goods returned.

Q1 What advice would you give to a shopper to help avoid disappointment?

Q2 In each of the examples below discuss whether the customer has grounds for complaint to the shop.

Q3 Why should complaints of faulty goods be made to the shop rather than to the manufacturer?

Q4 Why is it important to keep bills and receipts?

Q5 Should a customer accept a credit note for faulty goods? What are the alternatives? Which Act protects the consumer?

Further Steps

When complaining, if you do not get satisfaction from a shop assistant, ask to speak to the Manager. If a branch shop will not accept a complaint, you may write to the Head Office (address in the telephone directory), and explain the case. You should hold on to your receipt and send a photocopy if necessary.

Some **trade associations** lay down codes of practice, including complaints' procedures, and it is possible to write to them e.g. the Mail Order Traders' Association.

All **State Services** (e.g. British Rail or National Health Service) have users' committees to whom complaints may be addressed.

Local **Chambers of Commerce** are also concerned with good relations between trader and customer; their address is in the telephone directory.

Local authority officers should be contacted at the town hall to report cases of possible food poisoning or stale or dirty food sales (to the Environmental Health Department); or cases of false weight or description (to the Trading Standards Department).

Local **Consumer Advice Centres** or **Citizens' Advice Bureaux** will be glad to advise shoppers on what steps they should take.

The final step may be through the law courts. Larger claims have to be dealt with formally by lawyers in the County Court; and legal aid may be available. However, for smaller amounts (up to £500) the **Small Claims Procedure** is informal and you can explain your case yourself.

Q6 List the possible places you may refer to, if you do not get satisfaction on a complaint in a shop.

Vocabulary

British Standards Institution
An organisation which lays down desirable standards for the manufacture of many goods.

Chambers of Commerce
Associations of local traders.

Citizens' Advice Bureaux
Local advice centres which will answer enquiries, e.g. on housing, legal matters, social problems, etc.

Consumer Advice Centres
Local centres that advise on consumer matters, conduct retail surverys, etc.

Consumer groups
Local organisations which hold meetings for members interested in consumer affairs. They produce local shopping information.

Contract
Agreement between buyer and seller for the sale of goods or services which is legally binding.

Environmental Health Officers
Local inspectors employed at the town hall, who enforce a number of laws concerned with food, health and hygiene.

Kitemark
Symbol of the British Standards Institution which may be displayed by manufacturers whose products comply with BSI standards.

Merchantable quality
This means that goods are of an adequate standard, fit for their normal purpose.

Trading Standards Officers
Local inspectors employed at the Town Hall who enforce a number of consumer laws.

'Which?'
Monthly magazine published by the Consumers' Association. In each issue various tested products are compared for price, performance and quality.

Woolmark
The name and registered symbol of the Wool Marketing Board, which can only be used on goods made from 100% pure new wool.

13 Wise money management

A budget, for a person as for a nation, is the planning of spending against money available. This involves making sure that day-to-day necessities are covered, and finding out how much is left for pleasure and leisure spending. It also means looking ahead to future spending, and saving towards large items. Saving now is for the benefit of spending later.

Saving should be planned in two ways. First, the amount saved should be budgeted from money available now: how much saving is possible, and how much is desired will depend on individual circumstances. Second, each person should "shop around" for the best type of saving, from the many types on offer, to suit individual circumstances and plans.

Sections

Section 1

Budgeting

Once you are in charge of regular money coming in, income **budgeting**, or planning your spending, becomes important.

Not all your income may be free to spend. Nearly everyone in work has **compulsory deductions**, for Income Tax and National Insurance. These deductions reduce your full or "**gross**" pay to what you have left to spend, your "**net**" pay.

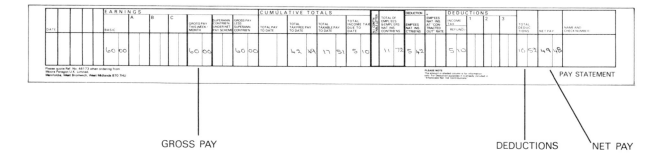

GROSS PAY   DEDUCTIONS   NET PAY

Your first consideration in budgeting must be to cover expenses of living and getting to work – rent, food, fares, essential clothes. Once these are provided for, spending for pleasure can be planned.

Each person wants to get the most satisfaction from what she spends. One may be keen on records, another on discos. Some may spend heavily on clothes, others on holidays. If you are saving for something you want, you may plan to do without some pleasure today for the sake of greater satisfaction tomorrow.

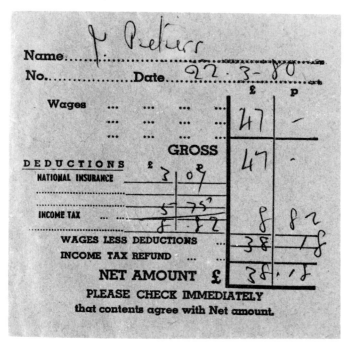

Q1 What is meant by budgeting?

Q2 Explain the difference between "gross" and "net" pay.

Q3 What compulsory deductions are made from earnings?

Q4 What are necessary expenses in each person's budget?

Q5 Under the broad heading of Living Expenses give three bills which a family would have to plan for, which might not be considered by a young person living at home.

Q6 Give five items of expenditure for a family under the heading "cleanliness".

Q7 Give five types of expense connected with a house.

Q8 List three once-a-year expenses for which you might put money by.

Impulse Buying

Some people plan the spending of all their income. Others are so careless and impulsive in their spending that they are always broke or penniless before their next pay packet. Impulse buying is a pleasure — to be able to take advantage of a bargain, or spend on the spur of the moment on something that takes your fancy: but it is a pleasure that needs to be kept under careful control!

Q9 What do you understand by impulse buying?

Q10 Have you spent on impulse recently, to buy something that you afterwards regretted? Discuss the reasons why you spent and what you thought later.

Q11 Describe a recent example of impulse spending that gave you real pleasure.

Q12 Describe examples of shop displays to tempt you into impulse buying in
a) a supermarket
b) a newsagent-tobacconist-sweetshop
c) a clothes shop.

Q13 Choose three particular items for which you might save over several months, e.g. a special item of clothing; leisure activities or equipment; furniture; holidays. Give your idea of the present cost of each item. Divide the total by six to show the monthly saving needed over half a year.

Section 2

Saving

If you are saving, you should consider what is the best method for you. There are many types of saving designed to suit different needs.

Some saving schemes pay interest **each year**, which adds to your annual income; others return a larger sum **at the end** of a longer savings period. If you want somewhere to keep your money safe for a short time until you spend it, then easy withdrawal — a counter service — is important. If you are going to save over a period of months or years, then you will choose as high a rate of interest as possible to help your savings grow.

Savings include all money set aside for spending later. Most saving schemes pay a fixed rate of interest; and your money is not at risk.

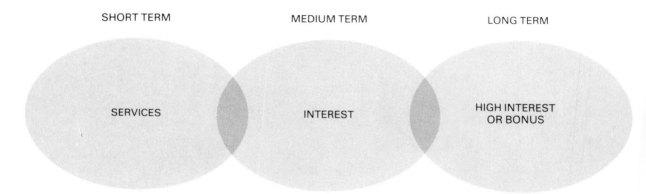

SHORT TERM   MEDIUM TERM   LONG TERM

SERVICES   INTEREST   HIGH INTEREST OR BONUS

Q1 Why should you "shop around" among saving schemes?

Q2 Describe circumstances in which you would prefer services rather than interest for your savings.

Q3 Describe circumstances in which you would prefer interest on your savings rather than services.

Q4 Describe circumstances in which you might have a regular saving plan.

Q5 What saving scheme provides the chance of a big win rather than regular interest?

Savings organisations

Many organisations are anxious to collect and use your savings for their own purposes. In return they are prepared to pay you, either by way of services (e.g. counter withdrawals) or with interest. The longer you leave your money with them the better it suits them; and if you agree to leave your savings with them for a fixed number of years they will pay a higher rate of interest, or a bonus at the end of the period. A contract for regular saving is also rewarded more highly.

Banks make a profit from lending money to industry, commerce and individuals. A **current** account offers a cheque book, counter services and others, but no interest is paid. A **deposit** account is for savings: it pays interest, but no cheque book is given with it.

Building Societies lend money on mortgages to house purchasers (see pp. 176–77). They offer a variety of savings schemes to suit different people. There is always such a demand for mortgages that they adjust their interest rates to keep money flowing in i.e. at a higher rate of interest than bank deposit accounts.

Savings Banks were founded to encourage savings among the working class, when few people had bank accounts.

The **National Savings Bank** is operated through post offices: and the money deposited with it is used by the government. **Ordinary Accounts** may be opened by anyone, from seven years old, with £1. Interest is calculated monthly. The account holder is given a **passbook** in which a record is kept of deposits and withdrawals. Up to £100 may be withdrawn without notice at any post office counter. The account holder's specimen signature is written on the front of the passbook so that it may be checked at any post office. However, it may be copied if an NSB book is lost or stolen and particular care should be taken of a passbook. Other services are offered, e.g., Standing Orders. **Investment Accounts** are designed for larger, longer-term savings. They may be opened by anyone, with £5. Because the money is left undisturbed a much higher rate of interest is given; but one month's notice of withdrawal is required.

National Savings schemes in a variety of forms are also offered for sale through the Post Office; and the money is used by the government.

Local Authorities are always in need of money for housing projects etc. They offer interest on term **bonds** i.e. units of fixed value (e.g. £100) repayable after a given number of years.

Life Offices collect and manage the premiums paid on Life and Endowment policies, and pension funds (see pp. 104–107). They are the largest collectors of "savings" in the country.

Finance Houses make a profit from financing hire purchase, and the commercial leasing of equipment and vehicles etc. (see p. 173). They offer high rates of interest for large amounts left with them for fixed periods.

There are also other savings schemes offered by different organisations, such as **co-operative societies**, and **savings and loan clubs**.

Q6 Name two collectors-of-savings where the money is used for the community as a whole.

Q7 Give two bodies that use savings to benefit members.

Q8 Give two savings schemes which encourage the saver to leave his money in for a longer period.

Q9 Give two types of saving that are encouraged by a higher reward.

Q10 Why are premiums paid on life policies regarded as "savings"?

Q11 Copy the diagram opposite, and under each circle give examples of organisations providing a savings scheme.

Q12 What is the difference between a National Savings Bank Ordinary Account and Investment Account?

Section 3

Savings plans

Jennifer Denvers feels happier with some money behind her, in case of a "rainy day". Whenever she can save £25 she buys a **Savings Certificate** at her local post office. After five years £25 would become £38.21 (8.85% a year interest, tax free). She could cash in each certificate with seven days notice, at any time.

John Maynard has a good salary now and can afford to save regularly. He has a standing order to pay £40 a month to National Savings on their **Yearly Plan**. The money can be withdrawn at any time, but earns the best rate of interest at the end of five years. This interest is free of income tax.

Peter Carey has a **With-Profits Endowment Policy** with a Life Office. It will mature or pay out when he retires, but in the meantime it gives his family the protection of life assurance.

Q1 Different savings schemes are offered to suit different people's circumstances. List three different types of saving that offer growth at the end of a period rather than interest yearly.

Q2 How much is a Savings Certificate; where do you buy it; and how long does it take to mature?

Q3 What is the benefit of a Yearly Plan?

Q4 Peter Carey is 50 in 1987, and retires in 1997. When would the life office pay out on his Endowment Policy
a) If he lived to age 75?   b) If he died aged 60?

"Anything we can save we put into a **Building Society**. Then they're more likely to help us with a mortgage, if we are already savers. We keep a number of different types of account. From our Ordinary Share Account we can withdraw money immediately over the counter at our local branch – and it's open ordinary shopping hours, and on Saturday mornings. Higher interest is paid on other accounts for larger sums so we have those for our long-term savings." Building Societies deduct income tax automatically from interest payments.

Mrs Allison has put her life savings (over £2,000) into National Savings **Income Bonds**. These pay her a monthly income, which helps her pension. Then after five years they pay a bonus, though she can withdraw money at three-months notice.

"We like the chance of a big win on **Premium Bonds**. Imagine winning £250,000! So I buy a £5 bond when I can, at the post office. There is a draw for prizes every week, and for a big one monthly. I won £50 last year."

Q5 Give three advantages of saving with a building society.
Q6 Why are Income Bonds attractive to a pensioner?
Q7 What is the advantage of holding a Premium Bond, and what is the disadvantage compared with other forms of saving?
Q8 What is the difference between a Premium Bond holder and a gambler, both of whom hope for a win?

Vocabulary

Bonds
A fixed sum lent (or saved) at interest.

Bonus
A lump-sum reward, e.g. paid after so-many years' saving.

Budgeting
Planned spending of income.

Building Societies
Organisations that encourage savings or deposits so that they may advance money against mortgages for the purchase of houses, flats, etc.

Compulsory deductions
Income Tax and National Insurance deducted from pay at source i.e. by the employer, from your "gross" pay.

Finance Houses
Organisations that pay interest to depositors in order to finance HP, credit buying and leasing.

"Gross" pay
Total pay before compulsory deductions.

Impulse buying
"Spur of the moment" spending, on a bargain or something that takes your fancy.

Life Houses
Organisations specialising in life or endowment policies and pension funds.

"Net" pay
Pay received after compulsory deductions.

Index